Lecture Notes in Computer Science   3475

Commenced Publication in 1973
Founding and Former Series Editors:
Gerhard Goos, Juris Hartmanis, and Jan van Leeuwen

Nicolas Guelfi (Ed.)

Rapid Integration of Software Engineering Techniques

First International Workshop, RISE 2004
Luxembourg-Kirchberg, Luxembourg, November 26, 2004
Revised Selected Papers

 Springer

Volume Editor

Nicolas Guelfi
University of Luxembourg
Faculty of Science, Technology and Communication
1359 Luxembourg, Luxembourg
E-mail: nicolas.guelfi@uni.lu

Library of Congress Control Number: 2005925572

CR Subject Classification (1998): D.2, F.3, K.6.1, K.6.3

ISSN   0302-9743
ISBN-10   3-540-25812-4 Springer Berlin Heidelberg New York
ISBN-13   978-3-540-25812-4 Springer Berlin Heidelberg New York

Springer is a part of Springer Science+Business Media

springeronline.com

© Springer-Verlag Berlin Heidelberg 2005
Printed in Germany

Typesetting: Camera-ready by author, data conversion by Scientific Publishing Services, Chennai, India
Printed on acid-free paper   SPIN: 11423331   06/3142   5 4 3 2 1 0

Preface

RISE 2004 was an international forum for researchers and practitioners interested in integrated and practical software engineering approaches that are part of a methodological framework and which apply to both new and evolving applications, technologies and systems. The ERCIM (European Research Consortium for Informatics and Mathematics) RISE working group selected application areas such as the Web, mobility, high availability approaches, embedded approaches and user interfaces in specific industry sectors comprising finance, telecommunications, transportation (avionics, the automotive industry) and e-government. Considered research issues in these areas pertain to the following software engineering domains:

- software/system architectures
- reuse
- testing
- model transformation/model-driven engineering
- requirements engineering
- lightweight formal methods
- ASE tools

All papers submitted to this workshop were reviewed by at least two members of the International Program Committee. Acceptance was based primarily on originality and contribution. We selected for these proceedings 12 papers amongst 28 submitted, and an invited paper.

The organization of such a workshop represents an important amount of work. We would like to acknowledge all the Program Committee members, all the additional referees, all the Organization Committee members, the University of Luxembourg, Faculty of Science, Technology and Communication administrative, scientific and technical staff, and the Henri Tudor Public Research Center.

RISE 2004 was mainly the supported by ERCIM, the European Research Consortium for Informatics and Mathematics, the "Ministère de l'enseignement supérieur et de la recherche," and by the "Fonds National pour la Recherche au Luxembourg."

November 2004

Nicolas Guelfi

Preface

RISE 2004 was an international forum for researchers and practitioners interested in integrated and practical software engineering approaches that are part of a methodological framework and which apply to both new and evolving applications, technologies and systems. The ERCIM (European Research Consortium for Informatics and Mathematics) RISE working group selected application areas such as the Web, mobility, high availability approaches, embedded approaches and user interfaces in specific industry sectors comprising finance, telecommunications, transportation (avionics, the automotive industry) and e-government. Considered research issues in these areas pertain to the following software engineering domains:

- software/system architectures
- reuse
- testing
- model transformation/model-driven engineering
- requirements engineering
- lightweight formal methods
- ASE tools

All papers submitted to this workshop were reviewed by at least two members of the International Program Committee. Acceptance was based primarily on originality and contribution. We selected for these proceedings 12 papers amongst 28 submitted, and an invited paper.

The organization of such a workshop represents an important amount of work. We would like to acknowledge all the Program Committee members, all the additional referees, all the Organization Committee members, the University of Luxembourg, Faculty of Science, Technology and Communication administrative, scientific and technical staff, and the Henri Tudor Public Research Center.

RISE 2004 was mainly the supported by ERCIM, the European Research Consortium for Informatics and Mathematics, the "Ministère de l'enseignement supérieur et de la recherche," and by the "Fonds National pour la Recherche au Luxembourg."

November 2004   Nicolas Guelfi

Organization

RISE 2004 was organized by the University of Luxembourg, Faculty of Science, Technology and Communication.

Program Chair

Guelfi, Nicolas   University of Luxembourg, Luxembourg

International Program Committee

Arve Aagesen, Finn	NTNU, Norway
Bertolino, Antonia	CNR-ISTI, Italy
Bicarregui, Juan	CCLRC, UK
Bolognesi, Tommaso	CNR-ISTI, Italy
Born, Marc	Fraunhofer FOKUS, Germany
Buchs, Didier	SARIT, University of Geneva, Switzerland
Dony, Christophe	LIRMM, University of Montpellier, France
Guelfi, Nicolas	FNR, University of Luxembourg, Luxembourg
Haajanen, Jyrki	VTT, Finland
Issarny, Valérie	INRIA, France
Klint, Paul	CWI, The Netherlands
Moeller, Eckhard	Fraunhofer FOKUS, Germany
Monostori, Laszlo	SZTAKI, Hungary
Pimentel, Ernesto	SpaRCIM, University of Malaga, Spain
Romanovsky, Sacha	DCS, University of Newcastle, UK
Rosener, Vincent	FNR, Henri Tudor Public Research Center, Luxembourg
Savidis, Anthony	FORTH, Greece
Schieferdecker, Ina	Fraunhofer FOKUS, Germany

Organizing Committee

Amza, Catalin	University of Luxembourg/DISI, Genoa, Italy
Berlizev, Andrey	University of Luxembourg, Luxembourg
Capozucca, Alfredo	University of Luxembourg, Luxembourg
Guelfi, Nicolas	University of Luxembourg, Luxembourg
Mammar, Amel	University of Luxembourg, Luxembourg
Perrouin, Gilles	University of Luxembourg, Luxembourg

Pruski, Cédric	University of Luxembourg, Luxembourg
Reggio, Gianna	DISI, Genoa, Italy
Ries, Angela	University of Luxembourg, Luxembourg
Ries, Benoît	University of Luxembourg, Luxembourg
Sterges, Paul	University of Luxembourg, Luxembourg

Sponsoring Institutions

This workshop was supported by ERCIM, the "Ministère de l'enseignement supérieur et de la recherche," and by the "Fonds National pour la Recherche au Luxembourg."

Table of Contents

Invited Paper

Integration of Software Engineering Techniques Through the Use of Architecture, Process, and People Management: An Experience Report

Christopher Nelson[1] and Jung Soo Kim[2]

[1] Siemens Corporate Research, Princeton NJ 08540, USA
Christopher.Nelson@siemens.com
[2] Carnegie Mellon University, Pittsburgh PA 15213, USA
jungsoo@cmu.edu

Abstract. This paper reports on the experiences of integrating several Software Engineering techniques by the Rapid Prototyping group of Siemens Corporate Research. This experience was gained during our recent project that involved developing a web-based, workflow-driven information system. The techniques integrated for this project included agile and iterative processes, user centered design, requirements discovery and maturation, and test-driven development. These techniques were integrated and supported by a proprietary process entitled "Siemens Rapid Prototyping" (S-RaP), a software architecture, and project management techniques. This paper will detail the specific characteristics of S-RaP, the software architecture, and the project management techniques that supported the integration of the above listed software engineering techniques. We will also report on our experience with their effectiveness and our thoughts on future enhancements in all three areas.

1   Introduction and Background

Siemens Corporate Research, Inc. (SCR) is the Research and Development organization of Siemens USA. Over the past several years, the Siemens Rapid Prototyping group at SCR has been developing, formalizing, and maturing an agile and iterative process entitled S-RaP. This process was born from the necessity to manage a series of projects that were emphasizing usability, as well as requiring the maturation of requirements throughout the development process.

To support projects with these characteristics, a process that incorporated User Centered Design (UCD) was fundamental for success. Unacceptable to our customers was a heavyweight requirements engineering phase, or for the addition of UCD practices to lengthen the time-to-market. In addition to requirements maturation and UCD practices, we also needed to include standard Software Engineering practices such as software architecture, design, and testing.

The rest of this paper discusses characteristics of the S-RaP process, architectural and design decisions, and characteristics of people management that we, at SCR, have utilized to combine multiple Software Engineering techniques. This

N. Guelfi (Ed.): RISE 2004, LNCS 3475, pp. 1–10, 2005.

combination has allowed us to include requirements maturation and UCD practices into our processes without lengthening time-to-market for the prototypes and products we develop.

2   S-RaP Process

The S-RaP process was designed and developed to aid in the execution of projects such as the one described in this paper. Key characteristics of these projects include a very short timeframe often in the order of 3 to 8 weeks from initial requirement capture to final delivery, vague and very high-level requirements that need to be explored and matured, and a heavy emphasis on usability.

The key aspects of the S-RaP process that allow it to successfully govern such projects, as illustrated in Figure 1, are that it is iterative, incorporates User Centered Design techniques, uses a single artifact throughout the life of the project that facilitates communication between the different process threads [9, 10], and executes three parallel threads of Requirements Engineering (RE), User Interface Design (UID), and Software Build (SB) [11].

2.1   Parallel Execution of Process Threads

By executing the three parallel threads of Requirements Engineering, User Interface Design, and Software Build in our process, we are able to integrate these three software engineering techniques in a unique way to help make our projects successful. Our process enables us to capture, over time, accurate requirements by allowing the requirements to mature throughout the development phase, as well as incorporating UCD techniques into our software development process. We have been able to do so without increasing our expected time-to-market.

The parallel execution of these activities is notably different from the serial execution of these activities, specifically in the coordination of, and communication among, the three threads in the process. With parallel execution, there is a need for a well-defined channel or mechanism of communication between all the groups involved. This is the case because parallel execution introduces a high risk of duplication of effort, or wasted effort from work done by one group in a direction inconsistent with the rest of the groups.

Our process incorporates the use of a single software specification artifact throughout the life of the project [9], as well as the functional prototype as a boundary object to facilitate communication between the groups functioning in parallel [10]. Also used to help mitigate these risks were short iterations, the co-location of all our team members and teams, and aspects of the architecture discussed later.

2.2   Short Iterations

All phases and threads in our process are executed in an iterative manner with very short iterations that are approximately one week in length. This serves several purposes. First, it ensures constant communication between all the groups

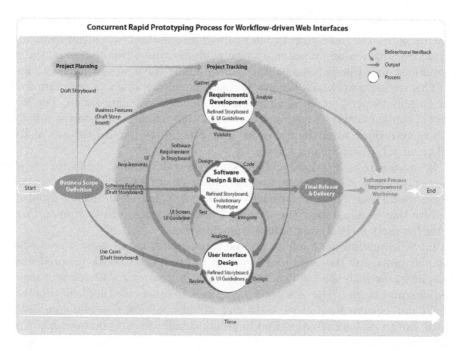

Fig. 1. Siemens Rapid Prototyping (S-RaP) Process Model

since inputs to one group for the start of an iteration are generated as outputs from the iterations of the other groups [11]. This is important to keep all groups in synch and to keep the team as a whole moving in a consistent direction as directed by our customers. Second, it allows each group to mature their aspect of the project based on feedback from the other groups. The RE team can mature the requirements by presenting usability feedback and the latest version of the application to the customer in design review meetings. The UID team can use the most recent version of the application as well as the newest version of the requirements to mature their UI definition and style guide, as well as continue usability testing. The SB group can continue to evolve the application's architecture, design, implementation, and tests based on matured requirements and UI feedback. Third, it allows for continuous usability testing, acceptance testing, unit testing, and market validation. This is important because of the dynamic nature of the projects. It helps to catch and fix issues as early as possible and acts as a safety net to protect against accidentally dropped tasks. This is very important due to the increasing cost of change as a project progresses [2, 3, 4].

2.3   Co-located Multi-disciplinary Teams

In our project we tried to maintain the co-location of our team members, and our teams. Our RE team was slightly distributed in the sense that two to three of the members were from our customer's organization which is located in a different state, and thus were not on site with the rest of the RE team. It is in this team that we notice the most difficulty in maintaining constant and fluent communication. For this reason we assign a single point of contact from our organization to our customer who is responsible for maintaining the flow of communication.

This seems to work well because it eases the burden of communication from our customer's perspective by eliminating redundant communication. The high level of communication stemming from co-located teams simplified the integration of everything from the use of an agile process, to parallel threads of RE, UID, and SB, to continuous testing.

In addition to facilitating communication, the co-location of multi-disciplinary teams also made it easy to put together sub teams of individuals with complementary skill sets. This was especially beneficial when we had difficult problems to solve that required expertise in several different areas such as Human Computer Interaction (HCI) and Software Engineering.

In such situations we found or noticed two methods useful, one for predefined complex tasks, and the second for emergent complex tasks. With the predefined complex tasks with specific deadlines, defining formal multi-disciplinary teams and assigning them to the task worked very well. In other cases, difficult problems would just emerge from other tasks and would not have concrete completion dates. In this case we often noticed impromptu hall meetings between members of the different teams. This was made possible by the co-location of the teams. In both cases, the co-location of teams really helped in integrating the UID team and UCD practices with the rest of the core team and practices.

3   System Architecture

The given business context of the project imposed a few significant risks on us that had to be dealt with on system architecture level. Multiple releases were to be made in sequence, and each release was tied to a very short timeframe with a strict deadline. Thus, we required parallel development of requirements and no-overhead integration. The customer did not have specific and concrete requirements from the beginning and usually asked us to demonstrate tangible and executable artifacts to get their ideas particularized. Moreover, the requirements changed frequently throughout the development. Therefore, we desired the ability to easily modify the existing implementation, at a given point in time, without breaking down the other existing parts. Yet, the user interface should be highly usable and consistent across different workflows and releases. Obviously development-from-scratch would not work at all under such circumstances, and a more structured and systemized design method was necessary. [6, 7, 8]

At the beginning we started with a very simple architecture of a client-server style and used MVC pattern [5] in the server. Throughout the development, however, we found the need for a better architecture that would facilitate dealing with the business constraints, and as a consequence, the architecture evolved. In this section we will explain the key aspects of the current architecture and its evolution throughout the development process.

3.1   Three-Tiered Style

Our system architecture is a typical example of a three-tiered style with a client tier, a server tier, and a database tier. The client tier is the simplest and thinnest tier of the system, consisting of a single standard web browser that can send HTTP requests and render returned HTML pages on the screen. The database tier is responsible for storing operational data, as well as providing a mechanism for read and write access for the data. The server tier sits in between the client tier and database tier. It recognizes requests from the client tier, fetches data from the database tier if needed, and provides results back to the client tier. Each tier is allowed to interact only with the other adjacent tiers through the specified communication protocol as illustrated in the Figure 2.

When the project was started there was no database tier, and the system consisted of a very thin client tier and a monolithic server tier. Throughout the development there were a lot of requirement changes, most of which are related to the UI requirements. We factored out the part of system that were not affected by such UI requirement changes and made it into a separated database tier.

This architectural evolution of logical separation facilitated application of several SE techniques to the project. Incorporating requirement changes was made easier because only the server tier was to be modified, leaving the database tier untouched or just adding new data objects without modifying the data access protocol. Macro-level testing was done more efficiently because each tier could be tested separately and independently. Especially the testing of database tier was conducted using the data access protocol without the server tier, and this eliminated a big source of defects, which reduced the time to locate and fix a defect dramatically. Also parallel development of a new workflow was done more systematically because UI parts and non-UI parts could be developed concurrently and integrated using the data access protocol.

For the design of the data model, we employed the actual object model from an existing Siemens product. Though it was an over-specified design, due to a few aspects of the data model that were not used in our development, we found this was a wise move because the overhead was from a product from which we

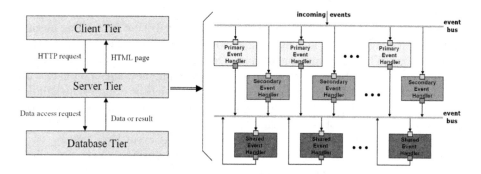

Fig. 2. Three-tiered architecture with hierarchical event-based style

could derive future requirements of our system. There actually were a few cases where we received new requirements from our customer, and the data support was already implemented in the database tier.

3.2   Event-Based Style

The internal architecture of the server tier is an instance of event-based style, which was a very natural decision because its job is to process asynchronous requests from the client tier. In other words, its execution is triggered only by the requests from the client tier, which are to be interpreted into events and processed in the server tier. Internally the server tier is structured as a collection of small event handlers, and each is responsible for handling specific events in specific contexts.

What distinguishes our architecture from general event-based style with multiple event handlers is that the relation between event handlers is hierarchical. Some event handlers have more privileges and responsibilities, but also some event handlers receive events directly from the client tier and selectively forward events to the other event handlers in the lower level of the hierarchy. Of the event handlers in the top level of the hierarchy, only one event handler is made active at any given point in time. The active event handler always receives incoming events, and is responsible for activating its replacement event handler when necessary.

When the project was started there was no hierarchy between event handlers. This was because each event handler was responsible for an independent portion of the requirements. This enabled easy allocation of requirements to developers. Throughout the development we found that there was a lot of redundancy in the event handlers that were implementing similar requirements. Such redundancy not only wasted our development resources, but also caused confusion and conflicts. The continuously changing requirements made maintaining consistency between redundant implementations a source of pain and defects. For the rapid prototyping we needed to eliminate that redundancy, and as a result we factored out common functionality from similar requirements into separate reusable event handlers that could be used by the originating event handlers. As a result the architecture was evolved accordingly to incorporate such structural changes in the design level.

For this reuse of event handlers we designed a unified event forwarding mechanism so that plugging in a new event does not cause any structural inconsistency or side-effects. Then, the implementation of an event handler simply involved filling in a template that already had the event forwarding mechanism built-in with the new functional behavior. Moreover, the internal details of an event handler were completely independent of the hierarchy of event handlers because event handlers have no way of telling where the events come from. The structure of the hierarchy was only important in the integration of event handlers.

This architectural evolution gave us a new edge in business. As stated, elimination of redundancy reduced the time for delivery. This gain has accumulated as we reused more and more through the development. The evolution also enabled easy assignment of requirements, and especially simplified integration. Since the event forwarding interface was unified, integrating a new event handler involved just plugging in a new software module. More importantly, the micro-level testing became more efficient because no redundant testing was required. Additionally, shared event handlers were previously tested thoroughly and believed to function correctly, which gave us more resources for testing new functionality.

This approach also enabled better requirement management. Since most functional requirements were captured as units of workflows and each workflow was implemented as a single event handler, the impact of requirement changes was localized and fairly small. Most of the time it was obvious which parts of the code should be modified to incorporate the changing requirements.

4   People Management

Along with process and architecture, we found that certain aspects of people management can also aid in the integration of Software Engineering techniques. The S-RaP process [11] discussed in section 2 leaves room for customization for different types of groups, teams, and people. This section details our experiences with customizations in team structure and methods for communication between the core team and the customer.

4.1   One Lead for Each Process Thread

We designated one team member from each of the three parallel threads of RE, UID, and SB to be the team lead for their respective group. This person was not to act in a project management capacity, but instead they were to function as a normal team member with two additional tasks of technical decision maker and designated communication channel.

This functioned very well in aiding the parallel execution of requirements maturation, software design, database design, usability testing, and functional testing. It did so by providing a common, well defined communication channel between groups, and reduced the potential for redundant communication.

This facilitated constant communication between all the groups, and allowed for inter-group decisions to be reached quickly. Since the lead has a bigger picture, decisions can be made with the consideration of other non-technical factors and release the burden of the developers to make "business" decisions based on the project schedule and the level of quality the project requires. The quick decisions kept groups active and productive by avoiding the down time that can occur when one team needs to wait to receive information from other teams. The communication also aided in keeping the teams synchronized. This was important because at the beginning of each iteration each team was dependent on output from the other teams' previous iteration.

4.2   Single Communication Channel to the Customer

Extreme Programming suggests having a customer on-site with the development team [1]. We agree with this idea, and feel that an on-site customer would be beneficial for all of our teams. However, it was not possible for us to have a member of our customer's organization on site due to the location of our customer's site and other projects that our customer was involved with at the time of this project.

Instead, we designated one member from our organization to act as a proxy. This person was a member of both the RE and UID teams, and it made sense to select her for this role due to the large amounts of communication that we expected between the customer and these two groups. The purpose of this designation was to funnel all communications to and from the customer through a common point. This helped us to present a single face to the customer, as well as keeping all groups in synch. This reduced redundant questions and answers, as well as aiding in avoiding conflicting information. The reduction in redundancy was beneficial to the core team, and made our customer's job easier.

Conflicting information can occur when two groups ask the same question to different members of the customer's organization and get two different answers. The reduction of conflicting information through the use of a single person as the interface to the customer was aided in following a process with several parallel threads while discovering and maturing the applications requirements. Even though an agile process with an abundance of communication can certainly help in discovering conflicting information early, avoiding conflicting information altogether is even better. The customer proxy was a member of the UID team, which enhanced integrating the UID team with the rest of the teams. It ensured the RE and SB teams were communicating with the UID team, even if the communication was indirect.

5   Lessons Learned

Throughout our projects we have learned several lessons we feel we should share with the Software Engineering community. These lessons regard customizing the software process, maturing requirements and software architectures, and risks involved with executing parallel threads during a software development process.

5.1   Software Process Improvement Workshops

One key lesson is that of process customization. Every software development process should be customized for specific projects, customers, team structures, and team member personalities. We made a practice of holding regular Software Process Improvement (SPI) workshops. These workshops consisted of brainstorming issues with our process, prioritizing the issues to surface the most critical, brainstorming solutions to the most critical issues, and then assigning ownership of solutions to members of the project team. We found that holding a SPI workshop once every six weeks kept the process maturing at an acceptable rate for the team members, without creating too much overhead or distraction.

5.2   Maturing Software Requirements

When maturing software requirements over the lifetime of a software project, it is important to pay attention to scope creep and to manage customer expectations. It is easy for the scope of a project to increase slowly as new requirements are realized, or as requirements become more complex. This is especially true when the requirements are being discovered and matured in a separate thread, parallel to the UID and software implementation threads. Sometimes the scope of the project can grow so slowly that it is hard to notice until it is too late. This can cause real problems when it comes time to deliver features to the customer. For this reason it is important to manage the customers' expectations.

We found that weekly design review meetings that allowed the customers to see the current state of development, as well as discuss issues with members of the RE, UID, and SB teams worked very well at keeping all parties involved in synch with each other. Developers and UI Designers were able to discuss and explain tradeoffs for different feature requirements to the customers so that the customers could make informed decisions about what would actually be implemented, without expecting more than could be realistically delivered.

5.3   Maturing Software Architecture

When allowing requirements to mature as a project progresses, the architecture will most likely have to evolve as well. Allowing for a software architecture to evolve creates multiple risks that must be planned for accordingly. One risk that we encountered was the speed with which the architecture was able to mature. Since we did not have an architectural design thread in our process, we left architectural decisions to our skilled development staff. Our development staff evolved the architecture as they received new and matured requirements. We found that if we did not task an individual to watch over the architecture maturation, the architecture started to evolve at a rate that was out of control. If a software architecture is to be matured during the development of a project, an individual should be assigned as a chief architect or technical lead to whom the responsibility falls to validate all architectural design decisions and to control the rate at which the architecture matures.

6   Future Work

So far, S-RaP is the only processes we have used with our highly dynamic projects. We intend to experiment with other processes. This will give us additional insight into how much we really benefit from the use of S-RaP.

We also need to explore the use of S-RaP for projects different in nature to the project described herein so that we can report on process customization. This could include a discussion concerning which portions of the process stay fixed, and which portions are variable.

Additionally, this paper reports largely on our experiences with regards to projects where highly variable customer requirements is the dominating characteristic. We feel that there are other important characteristics of Software Engineering projects, such as business and architecture complexity, but we were unable to address them here due to spatial limitations.

Acknowledgments

We would like to thank Bea Hwong, Gilberto Matos, Monica McKenna, Arnold Rudorfer and Xiping Song, as well as the other members of Siemens Corporate Research, Inc., consultants, temporary employees, and interns that helped make this project a success. We would also like to give a special "Thank you" to our customers who made this project possible.

References

1. Kent Beck: Extreme Programming Explained (1999)
2. Kent Beck: Test Driven Development (2002)
3. Ambler, S.W.: Examining the Cost of Change (2003-2004) http://www.agilemodeling.com/essays/costOfChange.htm
4. Ambler, S.W.: Agile Modeling: Effective Practices for XP and RUP (2002)
5. E. Gamma, R.Helm, R. Johnson, J. Vlissides: Design Patterns: Elements of Reusable Object-Oriented Software (1995)
6. Mary Shaw, and David Garlan: Software Architecture: Perspectives on an Emerging Discipline (1996)
7. Garlan, D., et al: Documenting Software Architectures: Views and Beyond (2002)
8. Len Bass, Paul Clements, Rick Kazman: Software Architecture in Practice (1997)
9. Hwong, B., Laurance, D., Rudorfer, A., Song, X.; Exploring the Effectiveness Potential of User-Centered Design and Agile Software Development Processes; CHI 2004, Workshop Bridging the Gaps between HCI and Software Engineering I; Vienna, Austria, April 2004.
10. Gunaratne, J., Hwong, B., Nelson, C., and Rudorfer, A.; Using Evolutionary Prototypes to Formalize Product Requirements. In the proceedings of: Bridging the Gaps II: Bridging the Gaps Between Software Engineering and Human-Computer Interaction; 24-25 May 2004; Edinburgh, Scotland; pp. 17-20. Copyright @ 2004 by IEEE
11. Hwong, B., Matos, G., Nelson, C., Rudorfer, A., Song, X.; People and Project Management Issues in Highly Time-Pressured Rapid Development Projects. Accepted to be presented at EuroSP3 - Cologne, DE, December, 2004.

Supporting Virtual Interaction Objects with Polymorphic Platform Bindings in a User Interface Programming Language

Anthony Savidis

Institute of Computer Science, Foundation for Research and Technology – Hellas,
Vassilika Vouton, GR-71110, Heralion, Crete, Greece
as@ics.forth.gr

Abstract. Today, there are numerous software patterns for the software engineering of User Interfaces through interaction object classes that can be automatically retargeted to different graphical environments. Such methods are usually deployed in implementing multi-platform User Interface libraries, delivering Application Programming Interfaces (APIs) typically split in two layers: (a) the top layer, encompassing the platform independent programming elements available to client programmers; and (b) the bottom layer, delivering the platform specific bindings, implemented differently for each distinct graphical environment. While multi-platform interaction objects primarily constitute programming generalizations of graphical interaction elements, virtual interaction objects play the role of abstractions defined above any particular physical realization or dialogue metaphor. In this context, a sub-set of a User Interface programming language is presented, providing programming facilities for: (a) the definition of virtual interaction object classes; and (b) the specification of the mapping-logic to physically bind virtual object classes across different target platforms.

1 Introduction

The notion of abstraction has gained much attention in software engineering as a solution towards recurring development problems. The basic idea has been the establishment of software frameworks clearly separating those implementation layers relevant only to the nature of the problem, from the engineering issues, which emerge when the problem class is instantiated in practice in various different forms. The same philosophy, when applied to developing interactive systems, means employing abstractions for building dialogues so that a dialogue structure composed of abstract objects can be re-targeted to various alternative physical forms, through an automatic process controlled by the developer. In the context of User Interface development, interaction objects play a key role for implementing the constructional and behavioural aspects of interaction. In this context, numerous software libraries exist, such as MFC, JFC, GTK+, etc., offering comprehensive collections of object classes whose

N. Guelfi (Ed.): RISE 2004, LNCS 3475, pp. 11–22, 2005.

instantiation by the running program effectively results in the interactive delivery of graphical interaction elements; such libraries are commonly known as interface toolkits. Currently, there are no similar libraries for abstract interaction objects, practically implying that their implementation and programming linkage to concrete interface toolkits has to be manually crafted by client programmers.

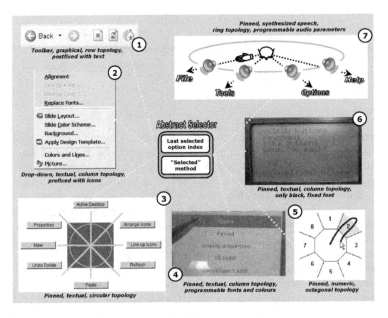

Fig. 1. Alternative incarnations of an abstract Selector varying with respect to topology, display medium, content of options, input devices, and appearance attributes. (1) and (2) are from WNT, (3) is from [3], (4) and (6) are from the 2WEAR Project [1], (5) is from [7], and (7) is from [8]

However, there are a few design models, in certain cases accompanied with incomplete suggested design patterns, as to what actually constitutes abstract interaction objects and their particular software properties. Past work in the context of abstract interaction objects [2,4,5,6,10] reflects the need to define appropriate programming versions relieved from physical interaction properties such as colour, font size, border, or audio feedback, and only reflecting an abstract behavioural role, i.e., why an object is needed. This definition makes a clear distinction of abstract interaction objects from multi-platform interaction objects, the latter merely forming generalisations of similar graphical interaction objects met in different toolkits, through standardised APIs. The software API of generalised objects is easily designed in a way offering fine-grained control to the physical aspects of interaction objects, since the target object classes exhibit very similar graphical properties. For instance, a multi-platform "push button" offers attributes like position, colour, label, border width, etc., since all graphical interface toolkits normally offer programming control of such "push button" object attributes.

In Figure 1, the large diversity of interaction objects supporting "selection from an explicit list of options" is demonstrated. Such alternative instantiations differ so radically with respect to physical appearance and behaviour, practically turning the quest for a common multi-platform generalised API, offering fine-grained programming control over the physical characteristics, to a technically unachievable task. However, as it is also depicted in Figure 1, from a programming point of view there is a common denominator among these different physical forms, which can constitute an initial design towards an abstract selector object. This abstract entity is concerned only with: (a) the index of the last option selected by the user; and (b) the logical notification that an option has been selected (i.e., "Selected" method). Since this entity has no physical attributes, there is still an open issue regarding the way fine-grained programming control of physical views is to be allowed when coding with abstract selectors.

Abstraction for interaction objects gains more practical value in domains where the implemented interfaces should have dynamically varying physical forms, depending on the interaction facilities offered by the particular host environment. Such an issue becomes of primary importance in domains like ubiquitous computing and universal access. Today there are no actual recipes for implementing and linking abstract interaction objects to different interface toolkits. In this context, we have implemented a User Interface programming language, i.e. a domain-specific language, encapsulating and implementing a specific software programming pattern for abstract interaction objects, while offering to the programmer declarative methods for the easy definition and deployment of abstract interaction objects. The next sections provide an overview of the programming facilities offered in the context of the I-GET User Interface programming language for the definition and deployment of abstract interaction objects - see [11], chapter 10, pp 120-151.

2   Definition of Virtual Interaction Object Classes

Abstract interaction objects are explicitly supported in the I-GET language through the keyword virtual, subject to specific deployment regulations. Therefore, abstract interaction objects are another category of domain-specific classes supporting compile-time type-safety. Definitions of key virtual object classes are provided in Figure 2. The source code for the complete definition of typical virtual object classes is surprisingly very small, while some of the supported features, such as the provision of constructor and destructor blocks are not practically needed. At the header of each virtual object class, the identifiers of the imported toolkits for which it actually constitutes an abstraction need to be explicitly enumerated, separated with commas. In Figure 2, the defined virtual classes are applicable to four toolkits, i.e., Xaw, MFC, Hawk (Savidis et al., 1997) and JFC.

In Figure 3, the physical mapping schemes of the State virtual object class are defined for the MFC and Hawk imported toolkits. The keyword instantiation issues the beginning of a specification block encompassing the logic to physically instantiate a virtual class to concrete toolkit interaction objects, through alternative mapping schemes. For each distinct toolkit, a separate instantiation definition has to be provided. At the top of Figure 3 two macros are defined. The first, named EQUALITY, employs monitors to establish non-exclusive additive equality constraints between two variables – see [11], chapter 5, Monitors. This is a more general approach than built-in constraints – see [11], chapter 6, Constraints, which upon activation supersede the previously active constraint on a variable. The second, named TERNARY, is used for syntactic convenience to simulate the ternary operator, not supported in the I-GET language. In each instantiation definition, there are arbitrary mapping schemes as subsequent distinct blocks (labels 1 in Figure 3), where each such block starts with a header engaging two identifiers separated by a colon (shaded lines in Figure 3).

```
#define ALL MFC, Xaw, Hawk, JFC          virtual Button (ALL) [
                                              public:
virtual Selector (ALL) [                      method Pressed;
    public:                                   constructor []
    method        Selected;                   destructor []
    word          UserChoice = 0;         ]
    constructor []
    destructor []                         virtual Message (ALL) [
]                                             public:
                                              string label = "";
virtual Container (ALL) [                      constructor []
    public:                                   destructor []
    constructor []                        ]
    destructor []
]                                         virtual Textfield (ALL) [
                                              public:
virtual State (ALL) [                         string Text = "";
    public:                                   method Changed;
    bool   State = true;                      constructor []
    method Changed;                           destructor []
    constructor []                        ]
    destructor []
]
```

Fig. 2. The complete definition of the most representative virtual interaction object classes (no code has been omitted)

The first identifier is a programmer-decided descriptive scheme name, e.g. ToggleButton, which has to be unique inside the context of the container instantiation definition, while the second identifier is the name of the toolkit class, e.g. ToggleButton, to which the virtual class is mapped (this need not be unique inside an instantiation). Even though the scheme name and the toolkit class name need not be the same, we have chosen to follow a naming policy in which the scheme identifier is the same as its associated toolkit class.

In each scheme, the programmer supplies the code to maintain a consistent state mapping between the virtual instance, syntactically accessible through {me}, and the particular physical instance, syntactically accessible through {me}Toolkit, e.g., {me}MFC or {me}Hawk. In this context, state consistency is implemented by: (a) the equality of the virtual instance attributes with the corresponding physical instance attributes, which is implemented through the monitor-embedding EQUALITY macro (see label 2 in Figure 3), or through explicit monitors when no direct type conversions are possible (see labels 3 in Figure 3); and (b) the artificial method notification for the virtual instance, when the corresponding method of the physical instance is triggered (see labels 4 in Figure 3). After all scheme blocks are supplied, a default scheme name is assigned, e.g., default ToggleButton or default RadioButton. Such a scheme is activated automatically by default upon virtual class instantiation, if no other scheme name is explicitly chosen.

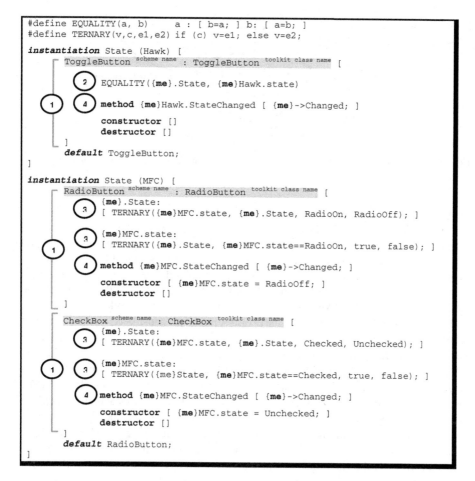

```
#define EQUALITY(a, b)     a : [ b=a; ] b: [ a=b; ]
#define TERNARY(v,c,e1,e2) if (c) v=e1; else v=e2;

instantiation State (Hawk) [
    ToggleButton scheme name : ToggleButton toolkit class name [
        (2) EQUALITY({me}.State, {me}Hawk.state)
    (1) (4) method {me}Hawk.StateChanged [ {me}->Changed; ]
            constructor []
            destructor []
    ]
        default ToggleButton;
]

instantiation State (MFC) [
    RadioButton scheme name : RadioButton toolkit class name [
        (3) {me}.State:
            [ TERNARY({me}MFC.state, {me}.State, RadioOn, RadioOff); ]
    (1) (3) {me}MFC.state:
            [ TERNARY({me}.State, {me}MFC.state==RadioOn, true, false); ]
        (4) method {me}MFC.StateChanged [ {me}->Changed; ]
            constructor [ {me}MFC.state = RadioOff; ]
            destructor []
    ]
    CheckBox scheme name : CheckBox toolkit class name [
        (3) {me}.State:
            [ TERNARY({me}MFC.state, {me}.State, Checked, Unchecked); ]
    (1) (3) {me}MFC.state:
            [ TERNARY({me}State, {me}MFC.state==Checked, true, false); ]
        (4) method {me}MFC.StateChanged [ {me}->Changed; ]
            constructor [ {me}MFC.state = Unchecked; ]
            destructor []
    ]
        default RadioButton;
]
```

Fig. 3. The logic for polymorphic mapping of the *State* virtual object class for the MFC and Hawk imported toolkits. The #include directives for the virtual class definition file, and the toolkit interface specification files, are omitted for clarity

3   Declaration and Deployment of Virtual Object Instances

The instantiation definitions for each different imported toolkit can be defined in separately compiled files, while being optionally linked as distinct software libraries, called instantiation libraries. During User Interface development, programmers have to link the necessary instantiation libraries with the overall User Interface compiled code. At runtime, when a virtual instance is created, it requests the realisation of its physical instantiation from every linked instantiation library (see Figure 4, step 1).

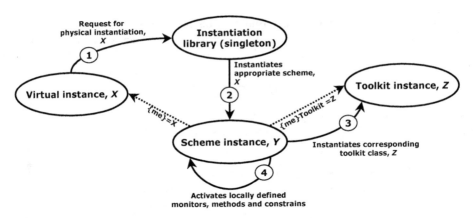

Fig. 4. The automatic runtime steps to physically instantiate a virtual class, for each target toolkit

As a result, each instantiation class, i.e., a singleton class, will create an instance of the appropriate mapping scheme (see Figure 4, step 2), i.e., either the default, or a scheme explicitly chosen upon virtual instance declaration. Then, the newly created scheme instance automatically produces an instance of its associated toolkit class (see Figure 4, step 3). Next, the scheme activates any locally defined monitors, constraints or method implementations (see Figure 4, step 4), which actually establish the runtime state mapping between the virtual instance and the newly created toolkit instance.

The resolution of the {me} and {me}Toolkit language constructs, in the context of scheme classes generated by the compiler, is also illustrated in Figure 4: {me} is mapped to the X virtual instance, while {me}Toolkit is mapped to the Z toolkit instance. As it can be observed from the above description of physical instantiation, a single virtual instance is always mapped to a number of concurrently available toolkit instances, this number being equal to the total instantiation libraries actually linked. In practice, this implies that, during runtime, virtual instances can be delivered with plural physical instantiations. For instance, if one links together the MFC and Xaw instantiation libraries, all virtual instances have dual physical instantiations for both Xaw and MFC. If the running User Interface is connected upon start-up with the respective toolkit servers of those imported toolkits, then the User Interface will be consistently replicated in two forms, at each toolkit server machine. A scenario of such runtime interface replication with two concurrent instances for windowing toolkit servers may not be considered to be particularly beneficial for end-users. However, if the interface is replicated for toolkit servers of toolkits offering complementary modalities to interactions objects, such as, for instance, the MFC-Hawk or the Xaw-Hawk toolkit pairs, then the resulting interface provides an augmented physical realisation of the application dialogue in complementary interoperable physical forms. Such interfaces can be effectively targeted to a broad audience including user groups with different interaction requirements, similarly to Dual User Interfaces [10], which offer a concurrent graphical, auditory and tactile dialogue delivery for both blind and sighted users.

```
#define PARENT(o) \
        parent(MFC)={o}MFC :parent(Xaw)={o}Xaw :parent(Hawk)={o}Hawk

agent ConfirmQuit (string text) [
        virtual Container   cont    : scheme(MFC) = FrameWindow
                                    : scheme(Xaw) = PupupWindow;
        virtual Message     msg     : PARENT(quit);
        virtual Button      yes     : PARENT(quit);
        virtual Button      no1     : PARENT(quit);

        method {yes}.Pressed [ terminate; ]
        method {no}.Pressed [ destroy {myagent}; ]

        method {yes}Hawk.Pressed    [ printstr("Hawk YES."); ]
        method {no}MFC.Pressed      [ printstr("MFC NO."); ]

        constructor [
               {msg}.label = text;
               {yes}Xaw.label = {yes}MFC.text = {yes}Hawk.msg = "Yes";
               {no}Xaw.label  = {no}MFC.text  = {no}Hawk.msg  = "No";
               {msg}Xaw.borderWidth = 4;
               {msg}Xaw.bgColor = "green";
               ...
        ]

        destructor [ ... ]
]
```

Fig. 5. An example of a unified implementation of a confirmation dialogue, engaging virtual object instances, retargeted automatically to the MFC, Xaw and Hawk toolkits

In Figure 5 an example is provided showing the implementation of a simple confirmation dialogue through virtual object instances. When declaring virtual object instances, programmers may optionally choose for each toolkit any of the named schemes supplied in the corresponding instantiation definition.

Additionally, since virtual instances are delivered with multiple physical instantiations, the corresponding physical parent instances have to be explicitly supplied per toolkit. For instance, the definition ok: parent(MFC) = {cont}MFC denotes that the physical parent for the MFC physical instantiation for the ok virtual instance is the MFC physical instantiation of the cont virtual instance. The I-GET language provides syntactic access to each of the alternative physical instantiations of a virtual instance through explicit toolkit qualification. For example, the expression {ok}MFC provides syntactic visibility to the MFC instantiation of the ok virtual instance, which, as it is reflected in the default scheme of the MFC instantiation, is actually an MFC Button instance. As it is depicted in Figure 5, virtual objects enable singular object declarations and method implementations, while also providing fine-grained control to physical aspects through physical scheme selection, physical-instance hierarchy control, and syntactic visibility of toolkit specific instances. The latter, apart from appearance control, allows specialised toolkit-specific method implementations to be supplied: see Figure 5, the implementation of methods {yes}Hawk.Pressed and {no}MFC.Pressed.

4   Code Generation

The support of virtual object classes having polymorphic plural instantiations, through facilitating scheme selection upon virtual instance declarations, is one of the most demanding and complex code generation patterns.

```
class _INSTStateMFC;
class _INSTStateHawk;

#define INST_ARGS   Agent*, _VICState*, unsigned, LexicalClass*

class _VICState : public VirtualObject {
        friend class State_Initializer;
        friend class _INSTStateMFC;
        friend class _INSTStateHawk;
private:
        static _INSTStateMFC*      (*instantiateMFC) (INST_ARGS);
        static void                (*deleteMFC) (INSTStateMFC*);          ①
        static _INSTStateHawk*     (*instantiateHawk) (INST_ARGS);
        static void                (*deleteHawk) (INSTStateHawk*);
        _INSTStateMFC*        _instMFC;                                   ②
        _INSTStateHawk*       _instHawk;
        MethodList            Changed_methods;
        SmartType<bool>       _VARState;                                 ③
public:
        void AddMethod_Changed (MethodFunc f, void* owner)
                { Changed_methods.Add(f, owner); }
        _VICState (
                Agent*       owner,
                unsigned     MFCscheme,
                unsigned     Hawkscheme,
                LexicalClass* MFCparent,
                LexicalClass* Hawkparent,
        ) {
④       _instMFC = (*instantiateMFC)(owner, this, MFCscheme, MFCparent);
        _instHawk = (*instantiateHawk)(owner, this, Hawkscheme, Hawkparent);
        }
        ~_VICState() {
                (*deleteMFC)( _instMFC);                  ⑤
                (*deleteHawk)(_instHawk);
        }
};

class State_Initializer {
        public:
        static unsigned flagMFC, flagHawk;
        State_Initializer (void);
};
static State_Initializer State_initializer;
```

Fig. 6. The code generated class definition for the State virtual object class; for simplicity, only the items corresponding to the MFC and Hawk target toolkits are shown, since for the Xaw and JFC toolkits, the resulting code generation is similar

```
static _INSTStateMFC* InstantiateMFC_Default (INST_ARGS)
        { return (_INSTStateMFC*) 0; }                           ⑥

static void DeleteMFC_Default (_INSTStateMFC* inst)              ⑦
        { assert(!inst); }

unsigned State_Initializer::flagMFC, State_Initializer::flagHawk;
State_Initializer:: State_Initializer {
        if (!flagMFC) {
                _VICState::instantiateMFC  = InstantiateMFC_Default;
                _VICState::deleteMFC       = DeleteMFC_Default;      ⑧
                flagMFC = 1;
        }
        Similar "if" blocks for all target toolkits
}
```

Fig. 7. The code generated implementation file (excerpts) for the State virtual object class

The runtime organization to accomplish this functional behavior has been illustrated earlier in Figure 4, introducing also the logical differentiation of classes among virtual objects, instantiation definitions and mapping schemes. Such logical distinction of roles is also reflected in code production, leading to the generation of appropriate classes from those three key categories. We will present the code generated for the State virtual object class of Figure 2, and its respective instantiation definitions of Figure 3. In Figure 6 and 7, the code generation from the compilation of the virtual class definition is provided. Overall, the code generation for virtual classes provides the ground for multiple concurrent physical instantiations, by delivering the place-holder as well as the activation mechanism for the toolkit-specific instantiation definitions. This capability to automatically activate any instantiation definitions of virtual classes, once their respective instantiation library is linked with the User Interface code, is the most demanding feature.

Following Figure 6, the produced header file encompasses firstly the forward declarations of the instantiation classes for each target toolkit, e.g., class _INSTStateHawk for the Hawk toolkit. The generated virtual class, e.g., _VICState, encapsulates pointer variable declarations for all potential instantiation classes (see label 2), like _INSTStateMFC* _instMFC for MFC. Additionally, all instantiation classes are defined as friends for the generated virtual class. The code generation for any local definitions made inside virtual classes is collected in one fragment (label 3).

Our approach towards automatic support for multiple instantiation, according to the particular instantiation libraries linked, is based on explicit instantiation and destruction functions pairs, e.g., instantiateMFC and deleteMFC (see label 1), one for each target toolkit, e.g., MFC. The implementation idea is that, initially, those functions will be supplied with a default empty implementation by the generated virtual class (see labels 6 and 7). Then, during runtime, each linked instantiation class sets, upon global data initialisation, its specific pair of fully implemented instantiation and destruction functions. To ensure that the pair set by such instantiation classes cannot be overwritten during initialisation by the default pair of the virtual class, we use a technique introduced in (Schwarz, 1996) for safely initializing static variables in C++ libraries. This technique uses a static flag per toolkit, e.g., flagMFC for MFC, which is to be unconditionally set by the respective instantiation classes after its specific pair of instantiation and destruction functions of the virtual class is set (this will be discussed later in the context of code generation of instantiation classes).

At the virtual class side, the default functions per toolkit are set only if the corresponding flag is not set (see label 8); consequently, irrespective of the order of initialization, the initializations made by instantiation classes can never be overwritten. Within the produced virtual class, those functions are called to actually perform the physical instantiation (in the constructor) or destruction (in the destructor) for each target toolkit (see label 4 for instantiation, and label 5 for destruction).

As depicted in Figure 8, instantiation definitions are generated as instantiation classes, e.g., _INSTStateMFC, while each embedded mapping scheme is produced as a distinct scheme class, e.g., _SCHStateMFCRadioButton. Scheme classes encompass two key member pointers, holding their runtime associated virtual instance and physical instance respectively (see label 1), e.g., myvirtual of type _VICState* and myphysical of type _PICRadioButtonMFC*. In the code generation of the scheme blocks, the compiler always resolves the {me} expression as myvirtual, and the {me}Toolkit expression as myphysical. As it can be observed from Figure 8, instantiation classes like _INSTStateMFC are very simple upon code generation, encompassing a super-class Scheme* scheme pointer (see label 2), which holds the particular runtime active scheme. Finally, the generated header file employs the technique for static data initialisation (see label 3), so as to ensure that schemes are safely initialized prior any runtime use (see also Figure 9). In Figure 9, key fragments of the generated implementation file for the instantiation definition of the State virtual class are supplied. As it has been previously discussed, scheme classes are responsible for the automatic creation of physical instances for their associated lexical class. Following this need, as reflected in Figure 9, the constructor of the_SCHStateMFCRadioButton scheme class (see label 1) firstly stores in the myvirtual member the caller virtual instance, and then performs the creation of a_PICRadioButtonMFC lexical object instance, stored in myphysical. The instantiation of the appropriate scheme classes is performed inside the constructor of the container instantiation class, through a switch statement (see label 2) over a parameter (e.g., the i) that provides the order of appearance of the desirable scheme within the instantiation definition. This number is easily defined by the compiler upon virtual instance declaration, being the order of either the programmer supplied scheme or the default scheme.

```
class _SCHStateMFCRadioButton : public Scheme {
     public:
     _VICState*                myvirtual; ]............( 1 )
     _PICRadioButtonMFC*       myphysical;
     Code generation here for constructs defined in the scheme block
     _SCHStateMFCRadioButton (Agent*, _State*, LexicalClass*);
     ~_SCHStateMFCRadioButton();
};

class _SCHStateMFCCheckBox : public Scheme { ... };

class _INSTStateMFC {
     public:
     Scheme* scheme;           ( 2 )
     _INSTStateMFC (Agent*, _VICState*, unsigned, LexicalClass*);
     ~_INSTStateMFC() { assert(myphysical); delete myphysical; }
};

class StateMFC_Initializer {
     public:                    ( 3 )
     static unsigned flag;
     StateMFC_Initializer (void); ]
};
static StateMFC_Initializer stateMFC_Initializer;
```

Fig. 8. The code generation of the header file for the instantiation definition of State virtual class for the MFC toolkit

Additionally, the compiler produces the key pair of functions for the instantiation (see label 3) and destruction (see label 4) of the generated instantiation class. Those functions are appropriately assigned upon initialization to the corresponding members of the virtual class (see label 5). After the assignment is performed, the corresponding flag is set, e.g., flagMFC, thus disabling overwriting of those functions with the default implementations due to virtual class initialization.

```
_SCHStateMFCRadioButton::_SCHStateMFCRadioButton (
        Agent* a, _VICState* v, LexicalClass* p
) {
        myvirtual  = v;
        myphysical = new _PICRadioButtonMFC(p);           ①
        Code generation here for initializations of constructs defined in the scheme block
}


_INSTStateMFC::_INSTStateMFC (
        Agent* a, _VICState* v, unsigned i, LexicalClass* p
) {
        switch (i) {
  ②           case 1: scheme = new _SCHStateMFCRadioButton(a, v, p); break;
              case 2: scheme = new _SCHStateMFCCheckBox(a, v, p); break;
        }
}

static _INSTStateMFC* InstantiateMFC (
        Agent* a, _VICState* v, unsigned i, LexicalClass* p   ③
) { return new _INSTStateMFC(a, v, i, p); }

static void DeleteMFC (_INSTStateMFC* inst)   ④
        { assert(inst); delete inst; }

unsigned StateMFC_Initializer::flag;
StateMFC_Initializer::StateMFC_Initializer (void) {
        if (!flag) {
              _VICState::instantiateMFC  = InstantiateMFC;
              _VICState::destroyMFC       = DestroyMFC;      ⑤
              flag = State_Initializer::flagMFC = 1;
        }
}
```

Fig. 9. Key fragments of the generated implementation file for the instantiation definition of State virtual class for the MFC toolkit

5   Discussion and Conclusions

Though the presented language constructs, the developer is enabled to define and instantiate abstract object classes, while having control on the physical mapping schemes that will be active for each abstract object instance at runtime; mapping schemes explicitly define the alternative candidate physical classes to physically real-ise abstract object class.

Polymorphism in virtual interaction objects	Polymorphism in typical OOP languages
• Aims to support alternative morphological realisations (i.e. polymorphism with its direct physical meaning).	• Aims to support re-use and implementation independence from different toolkits (i.e. polymorphism with its metaphoric meaning).
• Instantiation is applied directly on abstract object classes.	• Instantiation is always applied on derived non-abstract classes.
• Multiple physical instances, manipulated via the same abstract object instance, may be active in parallel at a time.	• References to an abstract always refer to a single derived object instance at a time.

Fig. 10. Key differences, with respect to polymorphism and abstract objects between general purpose OO programming languages and polymorphism as supported through virtual object classes

The need for having multiple physical instances active, all attached to the same abstract object instance (i.e. plural instantiation) can be exploited in case that the alternative physical forms are compatible, while their co-presence results in added-value interactions. For instance, in the context of Dual interface development [10], two concurrently active instances are always required (i.e. a visual and a non-visual) for each abstract object instance. The notion of polymorphic physical mapping and plural instantiation, have fundamentally different functional requirements, with respect to polymorphism of super-classes in OOP languages. The key differences are outlined in Figure 10.

Clearly, the traditional schema of abstract / physical class separation in OOP languages by means of class hierarchies and ISA relationships cannot be directly applied for implementing the abstract / physical class schema as needed in interface development. An explicit run-time architecture is required, where connections among abstract and physical instances are explicit programming references, beyond the typical instance-of run-time links from ISA hierarchies.

References

1. 2WEAR project (2003). Web site, http://2wear.ics.forth.gr, see Demonstrator pictures.
2. Blattner, M.M.; Glinert, J.A. & Ormsby, G.R. (1992). "Metawidgets: towards a theory of multimodal interface design". In Proceedings of COMPSAC '92 (pp. 115-120). Los Alamitos, CA: IEEE Computer Society Press.
3. Bronevetsky, G. (2003). Circle Menus. Demo implemented in Java, available electronically from: http://www.cs.cornell.edu/boom/2001sp/Bronevetsky/Circle%20Menu%20Documentation.htm
4. Duke, D., Harrison, M. (1993). Abstract Interaction Objects. Computer Graphics Forum, 12 (3), 1993, 25-36.
5. Duke, D., Faconti, G., Harrison, M., Paterno, F. (1994). Unifying view of interactors. Amodeus Project Document: SM/WP18, 1994.
6. Foley, J., Van Dam, A. (1983). Fundamentals fo interactive computer graphics. Addison-Wesley Publishing, 1983 (1st edition), 137-179.
7. McGuffin, M., Burtnyk, N., Kurtenbach, G. (2001). FaST Sliders: Integrating Marking Menus and the Adjustment of Continuous Values. Graphics Interface 2001, paper available online from: http://www.graphicsinterface.org/cgi-bin/DownloadPaper?name=2002/174/paper174.pdf.
8. Savidis, A., Stephanidis, C., Korte, A., Crispien, K., Fellbaum, K. (1996). A Generic Direct-Manipulation 3D-Auditory Environment for Hierarchical Navigation in Non-visual Interaction. In proceedings of the ACM ASSETS'96 conference, Vancouver, Canada, April 11-12, 1996, 117-123.
9. Savidis, A., Stergiou, A., & Stephanidis, C. (1997). Generic Containers for Metaphor Fusion in Non-Visual Interaction: The HAWK Interface Toolkit. In Proceedings of the 6th International Conference on Man-Machine Interaction Intelligent Systems in Business (INTERFACES '97), Montpellier, France, 28-30 May (pp. 194-196).
10. Savidis, A., & Stephanidis, C. (1998). The HOMER UIMS for Dual User Interface Development: Fusing Visual and Non-visual Interactions. International Journal of Interacting with Computers, 11 (2), 173-209.
11. Savidis, A. (2004). The I-GET User Interface Programming Language: User's Guide, Technical Report 332, ICS-FORTH, January 2004, available electronically from: ftp://ftp.ics.forth.gr/tech-reports/2004/2004.TR332.I-ET_User_Interface_Programming_Language.pdf
12. Schwarz, J. (1996). *Initialising static variables in C++ libraries*. In C++ Gems, Lippman, S. (Ed), SIGS Books, New York, pp 237-241.

Towards a Methodology for Component-Driven Design

Colin Atkinson and Oliver Hummel

University of Mannheim, Chair of Software Technology,
68161 Mannheim, Germany
{atkinson, hummel}@informatik.uni-mannheim.de
http://swt.informatik.uni-mannheim.de

Abstract. Component-based development has yet to make a big impact in software engineering as it has in other engineering disciplines because the components available for reuse are relatively much more primitive. This means that reused components usually account for a much smaller proportion of the overall intellectual effort invested in new software products than they do in other kinds of products. To rectify this situation more advanced development methodologies are required that encourage and enable software engineers to exploit richer software components – sometimes called "business" components – in the development of new applications. This, in turn, requires more advanced techniques for specifying and retrieving prefabricated components. In this paper we present some initial steps towards such a methodology based on the integration of two independent but complementary technologies – model-based component modeling and test-driven component harvesting.

1 Introduction

Ever since Konrad Zuse developed the first programming language, Plankalkül [1], in the 1940's, engineers have been striving to make software development more like other engineering disciplines in which new products are created primarily by assembling standardized parts. When automotive engineers design new cars or electronic engineers design new computers they don't have to develop every part of the new product from the ground up but they instead combine domain components such as engines and computer chips etc. in new ways. Moreover, these components are relatively complex, and thus account for a large percent of the intellectual knowledge and work that goes into the overall product.

When using a high level programming language such as Java or C# to develop a new application, programmers are essentially combining the primitive "components" provided by the programming language and its class libraries. However, these are much more primitive than the components used in other engineering disciplines. Building software applications from statement-level components is akin to building a computer at the level of transistors and gates. The net effect is that in software applications, reused components account for a much lower fraction of the overall intellectual effort involved in building a complete product.

To reduce the proportion of "new" intellectual effort involved in creating software applications it is necessary to assemble them from larger, more functionally rich com-

N. Guelfi (Ed.): RISE 2004, LNCS 3475, pp. 23–33, 2005.

ponents than those typically found in programming languages and class libraries today[1]. This, in turn, implies the need for a new generation of methodologies which do a much better job in encouraging and enabling software engineers to reuse behavior rich business components in new applications. Such methodologies must make developers aware of the existence of business components (and hence of the potential to reuse them) immediately at the point when creative design decisions are made, not when low-level implementation or deployment issues are resolved. Software systems could then be architected to take advantage of the existing components just as cars and computers are today.

Two main obstacles currently stand in the way of this vision, however. The first is the lack of standardized ways to create semantically complete descriptions of rich business components, and the second is the lack of effective ways for identifying suitable components that satisfy these descriptions. Today's state-of-the-art component technologies – namely, CORBA [16], J2EE [17], .NET [18] and Web Services [19] – have major shortcomings in both of these regards. Their interface representation techniques all basically focus on the description of the syntactic interface of the services (i.e. functions) offered by components, but gives very little information about the data models (i.e. ontology) or the states spaces possessed by components. Similarly, their component "finding" capabilities, to the extent that they provide any, consists of a "lookup" service in which components are registered for subsequent discovery by a manual or text based match. However, there is little support for the automated discovery of component based on their semantics.

In this paper we describe how it is possible to address some of these problems by integrating two complementary technologies for describing and finding components – a technique for model-based component modeling based on KobrA [4] and a technique for test-driven component harvesting known as Extreme Harvesting [9]. After giving a brief overview of the two approaches in the following two sections, we explain in section 4 how they can be integrated to provide a methodology which encourages and enables software engineers to exploit richer software components in the development of new applications.

2   Model-Driven, Component-Based Development

As its name implies, a component is an independent part of a product or system which has the potential to be used elsewhere independently [5]. In the context of software development this idea has traditionally been associated with platform and middleware technologies such as CORBA, EJB and .NET, with Web Services having joined this list over the last few years. Although these do indeed allow developers to package software into units that can be reused elsewhere independently, they do so only at the relatively low "implementation" level of abstraction once all the important architectural decisions have been made. In order to gain the full reuse benefits of the component concept, however, it is necessary to exploit existing components in the earlier analysis and design phases where most of the creative design decisions are made.

---

[1] A term sometimes used to refer to such components is "business components".

Supporting the modeling of components during analysis and design involves more than just using UML component diagrams to document the static interfaces of components. On the contrary, a component-based design must describe all the varied properties of components and their interactions at both run-time and development time. Component-based design thus involves the use of many UML diagrams to provide multiple, interconnected views of a component's different facets.

Although several methods support component-based design in one form or another, we base our approach in this paper on the KobrA method [4] since this has one of the most complete approaches to the modeling of components. The basic idea governing the use of the UML in KobrA is that individual diagrams should focus on the description of the properties of an individual component. In KobrA this is known as the principle of locality. Fig. 1 shows how a rich business component is modeled in KobrA by means of a suite of tightly related UML diagrams.

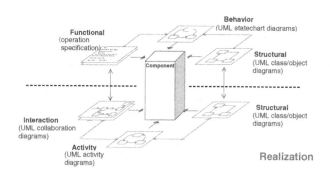

Fig. 1. KobrA Component Model Suite

The specification diagrams collectively define the externally visible properties of the component, and thus in a general sense can be viewed as representing its interface. The structural diagram describes the types which the component manipulates, the other components with which it interacts and the list of services and attributes which it exports. The functional model provides a declarative description of each of the services or operations supported by the component in terms of pre- and post- conditions. Finally, the behavioral model describes the externally visible (i.e. logical states) exhibited by the component.

The realization diagrams collectively define how the component realizes its specifications in terms of interactions with other components and objects. This can include externally acquired server components, or subcomponents which the component creates and manages itself. The realization diagrams collectively describe the architecture and/or design of the component. The structural diagram is a refinement of the specification structural diagram which includes the additional types and roles needed to realize the component. The interaction diagrams document how each operation of the component is realized in terms of interactions with other components and objects. Finally, the activity diagrams documents the algorithm used to realize each operation.

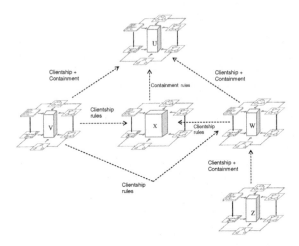

Fig. 2. KobrA Component Containment Tree

A complete model driven architecture of a system is created in KobrA by hierarchically organizing the models of the individual components which it contains. The hierarchy of component is determined by the logical containment structure as illustrated in Fig. 2. The system is regarded as the root of the containment tree. Its services are utilized by the users, and the subcomponents that form part of its realization are documented in the same way as children in the containment hierarchy.

To give a small example of how this approach is used in practice the following three figures give sample specification models for a Stack component. Although this is a very simple kind of component, the example shows how different UML diagrams are used in KobrA to capture distinct facets of a component as a unified abstraction. Fig. 3 shows the information or structural model of the Stack component. The diagram shows that a stack has two methods, push() and pop(), two logical attributes, max and elements, and stores instances of the class Object. This defines all the structural information (no more and no less) that a user of the Stack needs to know in order to use it successfully.

Fig. 3. Stack Component Information Model

Fig. 4 shows the specification of an individual operation of the stack – the push() method - in terms of pre and post conditions. The *Assumes* clause is the precondition which states that a stack object must not be full if the push() method is to execute successfully. The *Result* clause is the post condition which describes what effects a successfully execution of the operation has in terms of the concepts in the structural model. The other clauses provide auxiliary information such as the signature and parameters of the operation. The collection of operation specifications (one for each operations of the component) represents the functional model of the component.

Name	push
Informal Description	An object is pushed onto the Stack
Receives	An Object o
Assumes	Stack is not full
Result	Object o is on the top of the stack

Fig. 4. Push Operation Specification

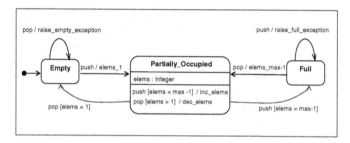

Fig. 5. Stack Component Behavioral Model

Fig. 5 completes the specification of the stack by documenting its behavioral properties in terms of the externally visible states and state transitions.

These three models (structural, functional and behavioral) provide a minimal yet complete specification of the stack component's externally visible properties. If any feature from any one of these models is missed out, vital information about the component is missing, whereas the addition of additional features provides no further information about how to use the component. This style of documenting interfaces using pre- and post-condition is sometimes referred to as design by contract [3].

3 Test-Driven Component Harvesting

Having described the component specification element of the approach, in this section we introduce the component retrieval element. A fair number of techniques for retrieving components have been proposed over the years, and it is not easy to categorize them because many overlap with one another. Mili et al [10] identify the following three more-or-less orthogonal categories of retrieval approaches:

- text-based retrieval
- lexical descriptor-based retrieval
- specification-based retrieval

Text-based retrieval approaches are essentially adapted from well known information retrieval techniques, with all the attendant advantages and disadvantages [11]. Searches are based on the textual representations of class and method names and textual descriptions of components (e.g. comments). This has the advantage that searches are not difficult to formulate. However, it has the disadvantage that the results are often too fuzzy to be usable due to the inherent ambiguity of natural language.

The second approach characterizes the functionality of components in terms of a set of key phrases from a predefined vocabulary. Although a great deal of effort is involved in defining the required vocabulary and annotating components with the appropriate keys, this approach is essentially the foundation of the ontology based knowledge representation technology use in the web service community [12]. The basic idea is to describe and retrieve components using descriptions of properties organized in inheritance hierarchies. Simple descriptions can be combined with Boolean expressions to attain better precision. However, a major drawback of the approach is the high level of skill needed to avoid building ontologies that are too general or too large for the job in hand. Because this is highly subjective, there is still no universally accepted ontology for service modeling.

The third category of approaches, specification based approaches, can be split into two groups depending on whether they provide a syntactic or a semantic description of components. The foundation for the syntactic approaches was laid down in the work of Zaremski and Wing on signature matching [13]. In this paper they describe techniques for the exact matching of function signatures and for partial matching using concepts such as subtyping to establish conformance relationships. Since the signatures of a component's operations can be automatically derived from its source code or binary code this approach is relatively easy to apply. The drawback is that pure signature matching only considers the syntactical part of a function.

The semantics of functions are usually described by using pre- and post-conditions which state what is valid before and after the execution of a function. The problem is to find a notation that does not introduce too much overhead and is also easy to apply. Unfortunately however, specification languages (e.g. Z [20]) tend to be highly mathematical and are thus inaccessible to many developers. The Object Constraint Language OCL [14], which forms a part of the UML suite of standards, is better in this regard but is still not widely used. An alternative way of checking the semantics of a function, at least partially, is the behavioral sampling approach suggested by Podgurski and Pierce [15]. This simply tests functions having the required signature with randomly chosen values and compares the output with the results calculated by hand. This idea has clearly some similarity with what we call black-box-testing [2] today but uses randomly chosen samples rather than carefully chosen test-cases developed according to some explicit coverage criterion.

3.1 Extreme Harvesting

Individually, none of the approaches described above provides a practical technique for retrieving components as part of a software engineering process. They all have at least one major weakness which limits their usefulness for finding potential reuse candidates during the creative process of software design. However, by using some of the techniques introduced above in combination it is possible to create a hybrid approach that overcomes some of these weaknesses and is capable of finding useful components during the design process.

This hybrid approach, known as Extreme Harvesting was developed to be as independent from specific component repositories as possible, since component repositories are expensive to set up and maintain and usually require developers to describe the components they store in proprietary or repository-specific ways [6]. In contrast, most techniques for the automated retrieval of components limit themselves to the mining of very specific (i.e. selected by a human) CVS repositories. However, such approaches are too limited to support a general reuse-driven design methodology so we decided to reuse some earlier Internet searching work [8] to investigate the use of generic web search engines like Google for searching components in source code form. Google is able to find about 300.000 Java source files and 100.000 C++ files in the web, so this is clearly a vast source of potentially reusable components. The problem is to find components that match a user's needs. Although there are several obstacles to overcome early indications are that this approach is able to find and deliver suitable components quickly and efficiently. Moreover, since there is no repository to maintain, developers do not need to add any extra repository-specific documentation to their software and therefore have no extra modeling burden. The disadvantages at present are mainly of legal nature because it is difficult for tools to automatically resolve licensing issues. Further discussion about this problem can be found in [9].

Most CASE-Tools today are able to create class frames of the following form from the class diagram in figure 3 and vice versa. Such a frame could be fed into a Java-based prototype tool that we have developed. We have omitted the stack's attributes here, since they would constrain the tool too much and are therefore not considered.

```
public class Stack {
    public void push(Object o) {}
    public Object pop() {}
}
```

Figure 6 below provides a schematic summary of the approach described above. In a nutshell it consists of six simple but complementary steps:

a) define syntactic signature of desired component
b) define semantics of desired component in terms of test cases
c) search for candidate components using Google with a search term based on (a)
d) Find source units which have the exact signature defined in (a)
e) Filter out components which are not valid (i.e. compilable) source units
f) establish which components are semantically acceptable by applying the tests defined in (b)

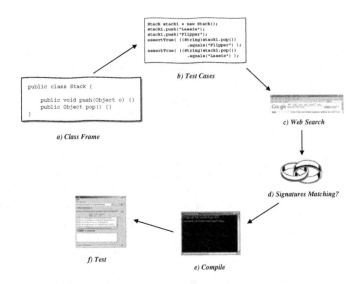

Fig. 6. Schematic process overview

This process has been implemented in the aforementioned Java-based prototype which is able to harvest components – i.e. source code modules that are directly pasted into a given class frame like that in 6. a) – from the web with just a single mouse-click after the developer has entered the desired method declarations and associated test cases. Our initial experience with the tool is very promising, e.g. we were easily able to harvest multiple implementations of our stack example, implementations of a class for matrix calculations and various sorting algorithms and mathematical functions. At present our prototype focuses on Java, but it can easily be adapted to other languages or web services. Even the combination of distinct languages is feasible when appropriate connectors – such as the Java Native Interface – are available, but we will not consider this here as it is beyond the focus of this paper.

4 Component-Driven Design

One of the reasons why the approach described in the previous section was called Extreme Harvesting was that it was originally envisaged as an enhancement to the eXtreme Programming approach to development. The creation of test cases to evaluate software units is one of the fundamental tenets of eXtreme Programming [7] – in fact, they are usually defined before the units they are intended to check. Therefore, the test-retrieval approach described in the previous section provides a natural complement to the regular programming-oriented way of realizing software units. Instead of programming a unit in the regular way, Extreme Harvesting opens up the possibility of realizing a unit by harvesting pre-existing source code from the web. As long as the unit satisfies the same tests a harvested component is theoretically equivalent, at least technically, to one developed from scratch.

While it can save a great deal of development effort, the drawback of this approach is that it focuses the reuse activity at the implementation level. eXtreme Programming, by definition, shuns a lot of up front design work and prefers to evolve the architecture over time by refactoring. However, this means that the reuse process and the architecture evolution process are disjoint from one another. The components to be retrieved and the software architecture containing them are designed completely separately. However, this is not the way in which product architectures are developed in other engineering disciplines. When developing a new product in a well established domains such as automobiles or computer hardware, engineers start off with a good idea of what kind of components are available and what kinds of architectures have been used in the past. The process of developing a new architecture for a new product is thus a highly iterative one, with ideas for possible architectures being developed hand in hand with the identification of possible components to realize them. Component-driven design is a highly iterative process, therefore, and requires a tight feedback loop between the component identification and component selection activities:

1. Model preexisting components,
2. Flesh out a potential first cut design, reusing already identified components wherever possible,
3. Model the interfaces of any new components featured in the design,
4. Search for new components matching these interface,
5. If perfect matches are found for all new components, use them,
6. If not repeat from (2).

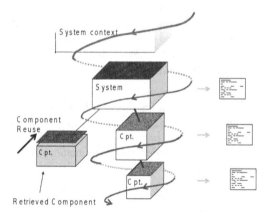

Fig. 7. Reuse Driven Design

The key ideas behind this process are illustrated in figure 7. The central part of the figure shows a hierarchy of components. Each component is represented as a box whose top surface is the component specification and whose bottom surface is the component realization. According to the KobrA consistency rules each subcomponent's specification must conform to the realization of the component containing it. In other words it must conform to the containing component's architecture. The canonical development process is top down as indicated by the spiral arrows in the center. However, the left hand side of the diagram illustrates that whenever a desired component specification has been created it is possible to find and integrate an existing component rather than to develop a new one from scratch. And this is where Extreme Harvesting comes in. It is the job of the Extreme Harvesting engine integrated into the development tools to find and present candidate components based on the component specifications and the associated test cases. It is even conceivable to use an extended version of our tool for the finding of components at runtime. The developer simply defines the syntactic and semantic interfaces of the required component and the tool can search the web or a web service registry for components that match.

But the real key advance in this process, and the reason why we refer to it as component-driven design is that the architecture is always developed or evolved with regard to the specifications that are known to exist and have all ready been defined. As in other engineering disciplines, therefore, architects have a pallet of existing components in front of them when developing the architecture. This contrasts with the situation today where architectures are first developed independently and then an attempt is made to retrieve components matching those required by the architecture. In component-driven design, feedback about the availability of components is provided as soon as a potential architecture to use them is modeled.

5   Conclusion

In this paper we have outlined a vision of a method and associated tool support which makes component reuse an integral part of the design (as opposed to implementation) process, and we have described two important foundation technologies for realizing this vision in practice - the KobrA method for component modeling and the Extreme Harvesting approach for component retrieval. We believe these provide a good foundation for a tool supporting component-driven design because –

1. the KobrA method emphasizes the up front modelling of software architectures and of the interfaces to the component that lie within them. This includes the development of functional test cases for the components, based on the specification models,
2. the Extreme Harvesting approach provides one of the most practical techniques for retrieving potential components which are both semantically as well as syntactically suitable for the requirements of the architecture.

We are currently in the process of adapting the Extreme Harvesting tool to retrieve components based on KobrA like models of components. As explained in the previous sections, once a suitable set of test cases is available the current version of the tool already has the ability to retrieve individual functions that satisfy the required semantic properties defined by the test cases. Applying this to all of the functions (i.e. methods) of a multi-method component is a trivial repetition of the process for individual functions. Checking the structural and behavioral facets of a component is trickier, however, but nevertheless possible as experiments prove. The former requires some kind of ontology matching or thesaurus based comparison of vocabulary and the latter requires some form of state machine based analysis of the desired and candidate behavioral models. Work is currently under way to address both of these issues. The one final issue that remains an obstacle to the development of a tool that really provides close support for component-driven design is the fact that at present the test cases have to be developed by hand. In KobrA this is seen as natural part of the component specification process. However, when an architect is in exploratory mode it is a burden to have to describe test cases by hand. We are therefore investigating techniques such as suggested in [21] to develop test cases from pre- and post-conditions.

References

1. Giloi, W.: Konrad Zuse's Plankalkül: The First High-Level 'non von Neumann' Programming Language, IEEE Annals of the History of Computing, Vol. 19, No. 2 (1997)
2. Myers, G. J.: The Art of Software Testing, Wiley (1979)
3. Meyer, B.: Design by Contract. In D. Mandrioli & B. Meyer (Eds.), Advances in Object-Oriented Software Engineering, Prentice-Hall (1991)
4. Atkinson, C., Bayer, J., Bunse, C., Kamsties, E., Laitenberger, O., Laqua, R., Muthig, D., Paech, B., Wüst, J., Zettel, J.: Component-based Product Line Engineering with UML, Addison Wesley (2002)
5. Szyperski, C: Component Software, Addison-Wesley, 2nd Edition (2002)
6. Seacord, R.: Software Engineering Component Repositories, Proceedings of the International Conference of Software Engineering, Los Angeles, USA, 1999.
7. Beck, K.: Extreme Programming Explained: Embrace Change, Addison-Wesley (1999)
8. Baumann, S., Hummel, O.: Using Cultural Metadata for Artist Recommendations, Proceedings of the Int. Conf. on Web Delivering of Music (Wedelmusic), Leeds (2003)
9. Hummel, O., Atkinson, C.: Extreme Harvesting: Test Driven Discovery and Reuse of Software Components, to appear in Proceedings of the International Conference on Information Reuse and Integration (IEEE-IRI), Las Vegas (2004)
10. Mili, H., Mili, F. and Mili A.: Reusing Software: Issues and Research Directions, IEEE Transactions on Software Engineering, Vol. 21, No. 6 (June 1995)
11. Baeza-Yates R., Ribeiro-Neto B., Modern Information Retrieval, Addison-Wesley (1999)
12. Hendler, J., Berners-Lee, T., Miller, E.: Integrating Applications on the Semantic Web, Journal of the Institute of Electrical Engineers of Japan, Vol. 122(10) (October 2002)
13. Zaremski, A., Wing, J.: Signature matching: A key to reuse, Technical Report CMU-CS-93-151, Carnegie Mellon University (1993)
14. Warmer, J., Kleppe, A.: The Object Constraint Language, Second Edition. Getting your Model ready for MDA, Addison Wesley (2003)
15. Podgurski, A., Pierce, L.: Behaviour sampling: A technique for automated retrieval of reusable components, Proceedings of the 14th Int. Conf. on Software Engineering (1992)
16. Siegel, J.: CORBA Fundamentals and Programming, Wiley (1996)
17. Matena, V., Stearns, B., Applying Enterprise JavaBeans: Component-based Developmnt for the J2EE Platform, Addion-Wesley, 2nd Edition (2003)
18. Lowy, J.: Programming .NET Components, O'Reilly (2003)
19. Kaye, D.: Loosely Coupled: The Missing Pieces of Web Services, Rds Associates (2003)
20. Wordsworth, J. B.: Software Development with Z, Addison-Wesley (1992)
21. Benattou, M., Bruel, J. M., Hameurlain, N.: Generating Test Data from OCL Specification, Research Report, Université de Pau (2002)

Automatic Translation of Service Specification to a Behavioral Type Language for Dynamic Service Verification

Shanshan Jiang, Cyril Carrez, and Finn Arve Aagesen

Department of Telematics,
Norwegian University of Science and Technology (NTNU),
N-7491 Trondheim, Norway
{ssjiang, carrez, finnarve}@item.ntnu.no

Abstract. Networked *services*, constituted by the structural and behavior arrangement of *service components* are considered. A service component is executed as a *generic software component*, denoted as an *actor*, which is able to download and execute different EFSM (Extended Finite State Machine) based functionality. The functionality of an actor is denoted as its *role*, while a *role session* is a projection of the role with respect to the interaction with one other actor. We propose an approach for verification of the services, based on interface verification techniques for the verification of the role sessions. The service component specifications used for actor execution are based on XML representations, while the verification of the role sessions is based on a *behavior type language*. This language has a sound theoretical basis, and is used to avoid "message-not-understood" errors. Rules are given for automatic translation from the XML manuscripts to this behavioral type language. This translation first makes projection to the role session, using hidden actions. Those hidden actions are then removed so a sound verification can take place.

1   Introduction

Networked *services* constituted by *service components* are considered. A service component is executed as a software component in *nodes*, which are physical network processing units such as servers, routers or switches, and user terminals such as phones, laptops and PDAs. Traditionally, the nodes and the service components have a predefined functionality. Concerning both the nature of nodes and the software engineering principles, changes are taking place. From being a static component, the service component can be based on generic software components, which are able to download and execute different functionality depending on the need. Such generic programs are from now on denoted as *actors* (by analogy with the actor in the theatre). The functionality of an actor is denoted as its *role*, while a *role session* is a projection of the role with respect to the interaction with one other actor. *Role* and *role session* need the power of Extended Finite State Machines (EFSMs) in order to describe a complex proto-

N. Guelfi (Ed.): RISE 2004, LNCS 3475, pp. 34–44, 2005.

col of interaction (which is not the case with most Web-based services as they are request-reply services specified as procedure calls).

There are basically two different approaches to service verification. One is to model the composite behavior of the whole service [Hol90], but it leads to state explosion and has limited applicability for complex systems. Another approach is the decomposition of the service system and isolated verification of the decomposed parts (new services that reuse existing components can take full advantage of this compositional verification). Within this approach we have the sub-approach focusing on the interfaces between the service components, with interface type languages [CFN05, LX04]. Most of these approaches use behavioral type systems [Nie95, NNS99, RV00], where a type specifies a *non-uniform* interface, meaning the set of operations (or messages) the interface accepts depends on the context. Indeed, this type is viewed as an abstract behavior of the component, and is used during compositional verification to ensure liveness and safety properties of the application. We aim for a quick compositional verification, restricted to the compatibility verification of connected interfaces. This will keep the number of states very low, instead of verifying the compatibility of the whole behavior of the components. We used the type language developed in [CFN05], preferred because of its high level of abstraction. In this setting, each component must satisfy a contract, which specifies the behavioral type of its interfaces; an assembly of components is sound if connected interfaces are compatible.

This work is part of the TAPAS project (*Telematics Architecture for Play-based Adaptable System*), which goal is to enhance the flexibility, efficiency and simplicity of system deployment, operation and management by enabling dynamic configuration of network-based service functionality. See [AHAS03] and the URL http://tapas.item.ntnu.no. We propose an approach to verify the services, based on interface verification techniques for the verification of the role sessions. We provide an automatic translation from XML-based EFSM service component specification to the behavioral type language applied. The projection process has two steps. First, make projections that preserve the binding between the role sessions related to each service component by using hidden actions. Then remove the hidden actions so a sound verification can take place.

The paper is organized as follows. The context of our service specification is described through the related TAPAS concepts (Sect. 2). The behavioral type language used in the verification is described in Sect. 3. Section 4 gives the methodology of translation. Related work and Conclusion end the paper.

2   Some TAPAS Concepts

Part of the TAPAS architecture relevant for the verification is illustrated in Figure 1. For a more comprehensive description of the architecture, see [AHAS03]. Concepts such as service, service components, actor, role and role session were defined in Section 1. The concepts of actor, director, role and manuscript are concepts from the theatre, where actors play roles according to manuscripts

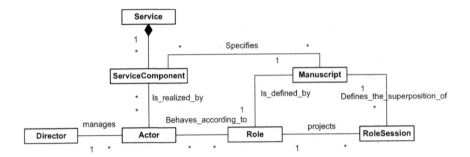

Fig. 1. Some TAPAS concepts related to the verification

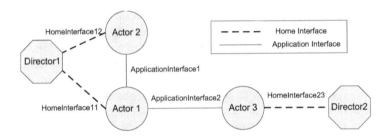

Fig. 2. Actor interfaces

and a director manages their operations. An actor has two kinds of interfaces (Fig. 2):

Home Interface. This is a control interface between an actor and its director. Each actor is associated with one Director, who manages the performance of the actor through this control interface.

Application Interface. This is an interface where the role sessions between actors take place.

Figure 3 shows the basic data structure of an XML manuscript. This manuscript is the specification of the EFSM based behavior of an actor. It contains the name of the EFSM, its initial state, data and variables, and a set of states. The state structure defines the name of the state and a set of transition rules for this state. Each transition rule specifies that for each input, the EFSM will perform a number of actions, and/or send a number of outputs, and go to the next state. The actions are functions and tasks performed during a specific state: calculations on local data, method calls, time measurements, etc. The <actions> list specifies only the action type (method name), parameters and action group (the classification of action types). This XML manuscript therefore specifies parameterized behavioral patterns. The detailed platform support and example implementation for XML service specification can be found in [JA03].

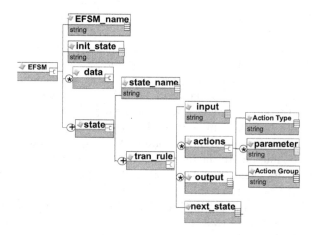

Fig. 3. Manuscript data structure

```
<state name="stInitUserInterface">
  <input msg="LogonEventInd"
         source="v_interface">
    <actions>
      <ActionType>ActorPlugIn
      </ActionType>
      <param>
        <name>role</name>
        <value>SchoolServer</value>
      </param>
      <ActionGroup>G1</ActionGroup>
      <store_return>v_server
      </store_return>
    </actions>
    <actions>
      <ActionType>setVariable
      </ActionType>
      <param>
        <name>value</name>
        <value>INPUT_MSG.school
        </value>
      </param>
      <ActionGroup>G2</ActionGroup>
      <store_result>v_currentSchool
      </store_result>
    </actions>
    <actions>
```
```
      <ActionType>setVariable
      </ActionType>
      <param>
        <name>value</name>
        <value>INPUT_MSG.user</value>
      </param>
      <ActionGroup>G2</ActionGroup>
      <store_result>v_currentUser
      </store_result>
    </actions>
    <output>
      <msg type="UserVerifyAccessReq">
        <param>
          <name>message</name>
          <value>INPUT_MSG</value>
        </param>
        <dest>v_server</dest>
      </msg>
    </output>
    <next_state>stPasswordIdentify
    </next_state>
  </input>
  <input msg="CancelEventInd" source=...>
    <actions>...</actions>
    <next_state>stInit</next_state>
  </input>
</state>
```

Fig. 4. Fragment of an example XML manuscript

A fragment of an example XML manuscript is given in Fig. 4. This fragment comes from an example application called TeleSchool, which we used as an experiment of our approach. For lack of space, we only show simplified behavior description for one state. This service component specification will serve as example to demonstrate the translation rules later.

3   Behavioral Type Language

We adopt the behavioral type language introduced in [CFN05]. This language describes messages that are exchanged on interfaces. We chose this language because it has a well defined semantics, and is based on a component model which is rather close to the Actor model of TAPAS. A component in [CFN05] has a set of ports. Each port interacts with a so-called *partner*, with which it sends and/or receives messages. Communication is asynchronous, and is made through an abstract communication medium containing FIFO queues (one for each port). A port will then be mapped to the interface in TAPAS, the main difference being that each port has its own queue, whereas in TAPAS there is one queue for the whole component. However, we think the two models are equivalent: retrieving, in a global queue, a message destined to an interface is similar to picking up the first message in the queue of that interface. The strong formal framework of the language in [CFN05] also allows us to avoid "message-not-understood" errors, and to ensure external deadlock freeness properties[1]. Moreover, a type not only imposes constraint on the interface it specifies, but also on its environment: it is possible to enforce the environment to send a message by specifying that the interface "**must** receive a message". Although this feature has not been used yet, we think it has an important impact on liveness properties when composing services.

In this paper the details of this language are not presented; the interested reader should consult [CFN05, CFN03], where a BNF table is developed, as well as semantics description and examples. However, we present an example of a bank account specification. The following type specifies the *operations* interface through which a client might perform credits and withdrawals:

operations = **may ? [**   deposit (real); **must ! [** balance (real); operations **]**
                          + withdraw (real); **must ! [**   balance (real); operations
                                                             + neg_balance (real); negbal_operations **]]**
negbal_operations = **must ? [** deposit (real);... **+** withdraw (real);... **]**

This type is read as follows: *operations* may receive (**may?**) *deposit* and *withdraw* messages. After receiving one of the two messages, the interface must send (**must!**) the balance of the bank account: message *balance* is sent when balance is positive, and the type becomes *operations* again. Message *neg_balance* is sent when the user is debtor, and then the type becomes *negbal_operations*. This latter type is similar to the *operations* type, with the exception of the modality: type *operations* **may** receive messages, whereas *negbal_operations* **must** receive messages. Hence, the client must perform some operations as long as he is debtor.

---

[1] The "message-not-understood" error avoidance is mainly due to the compatibility of the types of the interfaces. The deadlock freeness property is due to constraints on the internal behavior of the components, mainly on dependencies between interfaces (i.e. an interface waiting for a result on another one).

For the time being, we concentrate on the choice operator "+" and the sequence operator ";", so the resulting type is an abstract behavior of the component, which is roughly a projection of its behavior to a specific interface.

4 Translation Methodology

The actions that an actor can perform are classified into three types:

Control functionality through Home Interface: management functionality including `ActorPlugIn`, `ActorPlugOut`, etc., defined in [JAHB99]. A request is sent to the Director and the Actor must wait for the result.

Role session through Application Interfaces: the application interactions use asynchronous message sending through Application Interfaces.

Internal actions: they are invisible in the interface descriptions.

The translation from service specification to interface language uses projection. Projection is an abstraction technique, which can produce a simplified system description or viewpoint by aggregating some of the system's functionalities while hiding others. It has been used in previous works [LS84, Flo03] to simplify the verification of protocols and validation analysis. In our approach, the projection process basically consists of two steps. The first step extracts the inputs and outputs for a specific interface. All other actions are considered as hidden (internal actions and interactions occurring at other interfaces). The second step removes those hidden actions so a sound verification can take place.

The automatic translation algorithm is as follows. It scans the XML manuscript once and extracts the interface interaction information, the translation procedure being carried out state by state. Each interface has a unique identifier (for example I1), which is assigned dynamically when the interface is created. For each interface, every state has a type name assigned, which is composed of the interface identifier and a number. For example, interface types I1_* are used for all the interactions with the HomeInterface (Director), where I1_1 is the type of the first interaction, which will be transformed to I1_2 after some I/O interaction. This dynamic creation of interface type is flexible and easy for implementation. Each behavior description will be translated to the equivalent interface type description (using the translation rules described hereafter), affecting one interface at a time. Finally, gathering of silent transitions and states (Sect. 4.3) is applied on the interface type descriptions. In order to simplify the translation, each state will receive only messages from one single interface (i.e. all the inputs for one state are from the same source). If inputs are from different interfaces, we create new states for processing them. In our first implementation, **must** and **may** modalities are not distinguished: all actions will be "**must**".

4.1   Messages

In TAPAS, all communications are through asynchronous message passing. The input and output operations are the visible actions through interfaces and are translated directly into interface types. An input message means a receiving interface type "?", while an output message means a sending interface type "!". Synchronous communication can be implemented by an output followed by an input message, thus translated into a sending interface type "!" followed by a receiving one "?".

We consider only the types of the parameters, not their values. The resulting message types are then finite, so the validation will be a finite-state verification (our verification is an optimistic one: it does not handle the cases where values are received outside the scope of their type).

The XML message structures are input, output, and control functionality.

<input> structure. The parameter "source" identifies the role session, and distinguishes the interface for this input operation. This structure is translated to "?M_i", with M_i the message type.

Example 1.

XML manuscript	Interface type
<input msg="LogonEventInd" source="v_interface" >	I2_2 = **must ?** [LogonEventInd; I2_3] $I2\_*$ is used for the interface "v_interface"

<output> structure. The parameter "dest" identifies the role session for this output operation, and is used to find the binding interface. If it represents a new destination, a new interface will be created. This structure is translated to "!M_i", with M_i the message type.

Example 2.

XML manuscript	Interface type
<output> <msg type="UserVerifyAccessReq"> <param> <name>message</name> <value>INPUT_MSG</value> </param> <dest>v_server</dest> </msg> </output>	I3_1 = **must!** [UserVerifyAccessReq;I3_2] $I3\_*$ is used for the interface "v_server"

Control Functionality in <actions> Structure. This is identified by a method name starting with "Actor" in <ActionType> substructure. This should be translated to "! M_i; ? M_j" for the HomeInterface.

Example 3.

XML manuscript:

```
<actions>
  <ActionType>ActorPlugIn</ActionType>
  <param>
    <name>role</name>
    <value>SchoolServer</value>
  </param>
  <ActionGroup>G1</ActionGroup>
  <store_return>v_server</store_return>    <!-of type "roleSessionId"->
</actions>
```

Interface type:

I1_2 = **must** ! [ActorPlugIn (role); **must** ? [RequestResult (roleSessionId);I1_3]]
$I1_*$ is used for the interface "HomeInterface"

4.2   Deactivation of Interfaces

Interfaces can be dynamically created and deleted (deactivated). Deactivation is reflected by the "ActorPlugOut" control functionality. It plugs out an interacting actor, thus placing the corresponding role session into inactive state "**0**". The interface can then be deleted, the deletion being an internal behavior.

4.3   Hidden Actions and Their Removal

The first step of our projection on one interface replaces internal actions and interactions occurring at other interfaces by hidden actions, also called τ-transitions. The next step in the projection is to remove those hidden actions, by combining τ-transitions and states, as in Floch's work [Flo03].

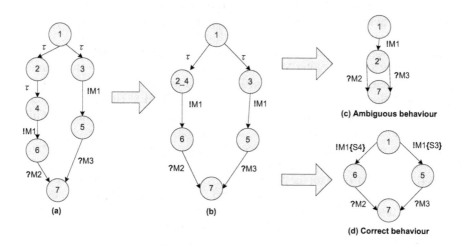

Fig. 5. Combination of τ-transitions

All the successive τ-transitions can be replaced by one single τ-transition, and the states are combined into one state, as shown in Fig. 5(b). If input and output sequences are the same for two states, these states may be combined. However, some ambiguous behavior may result, as shown in Fig. 5(c): from state 2' message $M2$ or $M3$ can be received, while originally $M2$ can be received only in state 6, and $M3$ in state 5 (This ambiguity may be due to some hidden parameter values, or to dependency between interfaces). We eliminate this ambiguity by adding state information in the name of the message (Fig. 5(d)): "! $M1\{S4\}$" means "output a message type $M1$ at the state $S4$". The final translated type for Fig. 5(a) could be expressed as follows, referring to Fig. 5(d):

I1 = **must** ! [$M1\{S4\}$; **must** ? [$M2$; I7]   + $M1\{S3\}$; **must** ? [$M3$; I7]]

$I1$ and $I7$ are the interface type description for State1 and State7 respectively.

As states and input types (messages) are finite, our types have finite states, thus avoiding the infinite state verification problem. We also provide a more accurate description of interface behavior than the traditional interface definitions, which specifies signature of methods but not complex interface behavior.

5   Related Work

Floch's PhD thesis [Flo03] provides a validation approach for dynamic service composition, which is similar to our work. Floch models the behavior of the service components as state machines using SDL; projection is used to transform it into interface behavior (also described as state machines using SDL-like notation). Our service specification has a higher level abstraction of behavior, as only action types are defined. Therefore, implementation details of the internal actions are already hidden, while at the same time keeping all the information about interface interactions. This simplifies the translation process. Another difference is that we provide translation by directly analyzing the XML data structure, whereas the transformation in Floch's work is based on state graphs.

The behavioral type language we used was first issued in [CFN03], and further developed in [Car03, CFN05]. Many type systems exist to capture the behavior of processes, actors or components, most of them based on process algebras like π-calculus. The closest type system to the one we used is the one of Najm et al. [NNS99]. The authors propose an actor calculus featuring regular or infinite-state behavior. Although they detect "message-not-understood" errors, communications are one-way. Ravara and Vasconcelos, in [RV00], were also inspired by Najm et al., but they did not make any distinction between inputs and outputs, hence their notion of error is rather loose and did not fit in our needs. They corrected this with Gay, providing so-called "session types" [GVR02], but distinguishing internal and external choice between actions (respectively client and server choices), which means we have to add messages to make sure those choices are made accordingly. De Alfaro and Henzinger provide another way of specifying interface behavior, using Interface Automata [dAH01]. Those automata specify the sequence of input/output allowed on an interface, but the compatibility they develop is too weak for our architecture. Indeed, two components are compatible if there exists an environment that can interact with the product automaton of the components' types; we believe this does not allow detecting "message-not-understood" in a plug-and-play environment such as TAPAS.

6   Conclusion

We have presented an approach for verification of the services, based on interface verification techniques for the verification of role sessions. We also provide an automatic translation from XML-based EFSM service specification to the behavioral type language applied. This language has a sound theoretical basis, and provides formal framework for compositional verification of component based systems. Especially, it allows us to capture "message-not-understood" errors while plugging a new component. The automatic translation provides an efficient and reliable way to extract interface types. An experiment has been carried out on an example application called TeleSchool.

For further work, the translated interface description can be used to compare specifications of behavior / service, so that dynamic service discovery can be done based on more accurate semantic interface behavior description comparison instead of simply signature matching. Furthermore, the dynamic assembly of components for validation needs to be further developed so as to provide safe plug-and-play techniques for components. Finally, we did not use all the features provided by the behavioral type language, and put aside the **may** and **must** modalities on the actions. We think about using the latter modality ("I have to send/receive") together with service-goal developed by Sanders and Bræk [SB04]: some actions can be specified as obligatory (**must**), so the service goal is fulfilled.

References

[AHAS03]   F. A. Aagesen, B. E. Helvik, C. Anutariya, and M. M. Shiaa. On adaptable networking. In *ICT'03, Proceedings*, Assumption University, Thailand, 2003.

[Car03]   C. Carrez. *Contrats Comportementaux pour Composants.* PhD thesis, ENST, Paris, France, December 2003.

[CFN03]   C. Carrez, A. Fantechi, and E. Najm. Behavioural contracts for a sound composition of components. In *FORTE'03*, volume 2767 of *LNCS*. 2003.

[CFN05]   C. Carrez, A. Fantechi, and E. Najm. Assembling components with behavioural contracts. *Annals of Telecomms*, 2005. To appear. Ext. of [CFN03].

[dAH01]   L. de Alfaro and T. A. Henzinger. Interface automata. In *ESEC/FSE-01*, volume 26, 5 of *Software Engineering Notes*. ACM Press, 2001.

[Flo03]   J. Floch. *Towards Plug-and-Play Services: Design and Validation using Roles.* PhD thesis, NTNU, Trondheim, Norway, February 2003.

[GVR02]   S. Gay, V. T. Vasconcelos, and A. Ravara. Session types for inter-process communication. Preprint, Dept. of Computer Science, Univ. of Lisbon, 2002.

[Hol90]   Gerard J. Holzmann. *Design and Validation of Computer Protocols.* Prentice Hall, November 1990.

[JA03]   S. Jiang and F. A. Aagesen. XML-based dynamic service behaviour repre-
            sentation. In *NIK'03, Proceedings*, Oslo, Norway, Nov. 2003.
[JAHB99]   U. Johansen, F. A. Aagesen, B. E. Helvik., and R. Bræk. Design spec-
            ification of the PaP support functionality. Technical Report 1999-12-10,
            Department of Telematics, NTNU, 1999.
[LS84]   S. S. Lam and A. U. Shankar. Protocol verification via projections. *IEEE
            Transactions on Software Engineering*, 10(4):325–342, July 1984.
[LX04]   E. A. Lee and Y. Xiong. A behavioral type system and its application in
            ptolemy ii. *Formal Aspects of Computing*, 16(3):210–237, August 2004.
[Nie95]   O. Nierstrasz. Regular types for active objects. In *Object-Oriented Software
            Composition*, pages 99–121. Prentice-Hall, 1995.
[NNS99]   E. Najm, A. Nimour, and J.-B. Stefani. Infinite types for distributed objects
            interfaces. In *FMOODS'99, Proceedings*, Firenze, Italy, February 1999.
[RV00]   A. Ravara and V. T. Vasconcelos. Typing non-uniform concurrent objects.
            In *CONCUR 2000*, volume 1877 of *LNCS*, pages 474–488. Springer, 2000.
[SB04]   R. Sanders and R. Bræk. Discovering service opportunities by evaluating
            service goals. In *EUNICE'04, Proceedings*, Tampere, Finland, June 2004.

A Symbolic Model Checker for **tccp** Programs*

M. Alpuente[1], M. Falaschi[2], and A. Villanueva[1]

[1] DSIC, Technical University of Valencia,
Camino de Vera s/n, E-46022 Valencia, Spain
[2] DIMI, University of Udine,
Via delle Scienze 206, I-33100 Udine, Italy

Abstract. In this paper, we develop a symbolic representation for *timed concurrent constraint* (**tccp**) programs, which can be used for defining a lightweight model–checking algorithm for reactive systems. Our approach is based on using streams to extend *Difference Decision Diagrams* (DDDs) which generalize the classical *Binary Decision Diagrams* (BDDs) with constraints. We use streams to model the values of system variables along the time, as occurs in many other (declarative) languages. Then, we define a symbolic (finite states) model checking algorithm for tccp which mitigates the state explosion problem that is common to more conventional model checking approaches. We show how the symbolic approach to model checking for **tccp** improves previous approaches based on the classical Linear Time Logic (LTL) model checking algorithm.

Keywords: Lightweight formal methods, Model Checking, Timed Concurrent Constraint Programs, DDDs.

1   Introduction

In the last decades, formal verification of industrial applications has become a hot topic of research. As the complexity of software systems increases, lightweight automatic verification tools which are able to guarantee, at little cost, the correct behavior of such systems are dramatically lacking. *Model checking* is a fully automatic formal verification technique which is able to demonstrate certain properties formalized as logical formulas which are automatically checked on a model of the system; otherwise, it provides a counterexample which helps the programmer to debug the wrong code. However, its potential for push–button verification is not easily realizable due to the well-known *state-space explosion* problem. Recent advances in model checking deal with huge state-spaces by using symbolic manipulation algorithms inside model checkers [7].

* This work has been partially supported by MCYT under grants TIC2001-2705-C03-01, HU2003-0003, by Generalitat Valenciana under grants GR03/025, GV04/389 and by ICT for EU-India Cross Cultural Dissemination Project under grant ALA/95/23/2003/077-054.

N. Guelfi (Ed.): RISE 2004, LNCS 3475, pp. 45–56, 2005.

The *concurrent constraint* paradigm (cc) was presented in [11] to model concurrent systems. A global store consisting of a set of constraints contains the information gathered during the computation. Constraints are dynamically added to the store which can also be consulted. The programming model was extended in [3] over a discrete notion of time in order to deal with reactive systems, that is, systems which continuously interact with their environment without producing a final result and execute infinitely along the time. The use of constraints, the inherent concurrency and the notion of time which lay in tccp permit to program reactive systems in a very natural way. Reactive systems are usually modeled as concurrent systems which are more difficult to be manually debugged, simulated or verified than sequential systems. In previous works ([8, 9]) we have defined an explicit model checking algorithm for tccp programs. Such method automatically constructs a model of the system which is similar to a Kripke Structure.

The main purpose of this work is to improve the exhaustive model checking algorithm defined in the last years to verify tccp programs. Starting from the graph representation of [9], in this paper we formalize a symbolic representation of reactive systems written in tccp. Such representation allows us to formulate a symbolic model checking algorithm which allows us to verify more complex reactive systems. To the best of our knowledge, this work defines the first symbolic model checking algorithm for tccp. In order to ensure the termination of our approach, we refer to finite state systems in this work. It would be possible to remove this assumption and consider infinite state systems by adapting to our context standard abstract interpretation techniques [2], or by requiring the user to indicate a finite time interval for limiting the duration of tccp computations.

The paper is organized as follows. In Section 2 we recall the tccp programming language and the tccp Structure which can be derived from the program specification and which is the reference point of this work. In Section 3 we introduce the verification method that we propose, and in Section 3.2 we define the algorithms that allow us to automatize the model construction process. In Section 5 we develop an example of property verification. Finally, Section 6 concludes. More details and missing definitions can be found in [1].

2   The tccp Framework

The cc paradigm has some nice features which can be exploited to improve the difficult process of verifying software: the declarative nature of the language ease the programming task of the user, and the use of constraints naturally reduces the state space of the specified system.

The *Timed Concurrent Constraint Language* (tccp) was developed in [3] by F. de Boer *et al.* as a framework for modeling reactive and real-time systems. It was defined by extending the concurrent computational model of the cc paradigm [11] with a notion of discrete time.

Basically, a cc program describes a system of agents that can add (*tell*) information into a store as well as check (*ask*) whether a constraint is entailed by such global store. The basic agents defined in tccp are those inherited from cc plus a new conditional agent described below. Moreover, a *discrete global clock* is provided. Computation evolves in steps of one time unit by adding or asking (entailment test) some information to the store. It is assumed that *ask* and *tell* actions take one time unit, and the parallel operator is interpreted in terms of maximal parallelism. Moreover, it is assumed that constraint entailment tests take a constant time independently of the size of the store[1].

Let us first recall the notion of constraint system which underlies the tccp programming language[2]. A simple constraint system can be defined as a set D of tokens (or primitive constraints) together with an entailment relation $\vdash \subseteq 2^D \times D$. Concurrent constraint languages, actually use a notion of *cylindric* constraint system, which consists of a simple constraint system plus an existential quantification operator which is monotonic, conservative and supports renaming. This additional operator allows one to model local variables in a given agent. The formal definition of the notion of *cylindric constraint system* can be found in [3].

In this work, we consider a specific constraint system which allows us to verify a class of software systems. In particular, we consider a constraint system with two kind of tokens: the first one allows us to handle arithmetical constraints whereas the other constraints are used for representing streams. In tccp, streams are modeled as lists of terms. These lists represent the value of a given system variable along the time. Intuitively, in the current time instant, the head of the list represents the value of a variable and the tail of the list models the future. The entailment relation for lists is specified by Clark's Equality Theory. For example, following Prolog notation for lists, $[X|Z]=[a|Y]$ entails $X=a$ and $Z=Y$.

We use $\mathcal{V}$ to denote the set of variables ranging over $\mathbb{R}$ (or $\mathbb{Z}$), and $\mathcal{LV}$ is the set of lists of such variables. From now, we will use $\mathbb{D} \in \{\mathbb{R}, \mathbb{Z}\}$ to denote arbitrarily one of the two domains. Roughly speaking, we define the set of tokens of our constraint system as containing the set of difference constraints of the form $X - Y \leq c$ and $X - Y < c$, as well as the set of stream constraints of the form $V = [\,], V = [X|W]$ and $V = [c|W]$, where X and Y belong to $\mathcal{V}$, V and W are in $\mathcal{LV}$, and the constant c belongs to $\mathbb{D}$.

We define the set AP of atomic propositions as the set of tokens of the (cylindric) constraint system above. In the rest of the paper, we identify the notion of (finite) constraint with atomic propositions.

Let us now recall the syntax of tccp, defined in [3] as follows[3]:

Definition 1 (tccp Language). *Let C be a (cylindric) constraint system. The syntax of agents of the language is given by the following grammar:*

$A ::= \mathsf{stop} \mid \mathsf{tell}(c) \mid \sum_{i=1}^{n} \mathsf{ask}(c_i) \rightarrow A_i \mid \mathsf{now}\ c\ \mathsf{then}\ A\ \mathsf{else}\ A \mid A \,\|\, A \mid \exists x\, A \mid \mathsf{p}(x)$

---

[1] In practice, some syntactic restrictions are imposed in order to ensure that these hypotheses are reasonable (see [3] for details).

[2] A formal definition of the constraint system can be found in [1].

[3] The operational and denotational semantics of the language can be found in [3].

where c, c_i *are* finite constraints *of* C. *A* tccp *process* P *is an object of the form* $D.A$, *where* D *is a set of procedure declarations of the form* p(x) :−A, *and* A *is an agent.*

The stop agent terminates the execution whereas the tell(c) agent adds the constraint c to the store. Nondeterminism is modeled by the choice agent (written $\sum_{i=1}^{n}$ ask(c_i) → A_i) that executes nondeterministically one of the choices whose guard is satisfied by the store. The agent $A \parallel A$ represents the concurrent component of the language, and $\exists x\, A$ is the existential quantification, that makes the variable x local to the agent A. The agent for the procedure call is p(x).

Finally, the now c then A else B agent (called conditional agent) is the new agent (w.r.t. cc) which allows us to describe notions such as *timeout* or *preemption*. This agent executes A if the store entails c, otherwise it executes B.

2.1   The tccp Structure

In [9], we provided a model for tccp programs which essentially consists of a graph structure. The main difference w.r.t. a Kripke structure is in the definition of the states. A state in a Kripke Structure consists of a valuation of the system variables, whereas in a tccp Structure, states are represented by (conjunctions of) constraints which represent a set of possible valuations of systems variables. In other works, a state of a tccp Structure represents a set of states of a Kripke Structure. In [9], the interested reader can find a formal definition of tccp Structures and a method to automatically build it from a given tccp program.

2.2   The Scheduler Example

In Figure 1 we show an example of tccp program which consists of a predicate with three output variables. We use streams to simulate the values of the system variables along the time. Intuitively, the program gets the value of variables D1, T1 and E1 by calling the process get_constraints. These variables represent the duration of three different tasks of the process of building a house. In parallel, an ask agent simply checks if the values of the variables are isntanciated to integer numbers and, in that case, some constraints are added to the global store. Finally, a recursive call to the building process is made which allows us to recalculate the planning schedule.

The tccp Structure associated with this code is shown in Figure 2. The black circle indicates the initial state of the graph. We have simplified the structure by

```
build([PD|PD_],[PT|PT_],[PE|PE_]) ::=
    ∃ D1,T1,E1 (get_constraints(D1,T1,E1) ||
    ask(atom(D1),atom(T1),atom(E1)) → (tell(PD+D1 =< PT) ||
        tell(PT+T1 =< PE) ||tell(PE+E1 =< PA)) || build(PD_,PT_,PE_)).
```

Fig. 1. Example of a tccp program

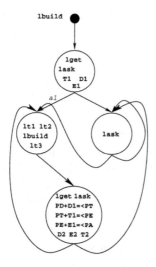

Fig. 2. tccp Structure of build

showing, in each state, only the new information added to the store. Informally, labels are used to identify the point of execution of the program. Each occurrence of every agent of a program is labelled, thus the set of labels in a given state represents the set of agents that must run in such execution point (see [9]).

The most important point of this example is the fact that we have added to the store only constraints of the form V1+C=<V2 which can also be written as V1-V2≤C being C an integer or real constant. This kind of constraints appears in applications where, for example, we compare two clocks of a system to control the timing between tasks, or in scheduling applications such as this example. In the following sections, we show how we can symbolically represent this kind of constraints in a similar way as *Binary Decision Diagrams* (BDDs, [5]) do in the basic symbolic model checking approach.

3   Symbolic Model Checking

The idea of symbolic model checking is to represent the graph structure (the model) as a boolean formula, and then transform it into the efficient structure of BDD [5]. In our approach, we aim to represent the tccp Structure as a formula with difference constraints and logical streams, and then transform it into a suitable extension of BDDs.

In [9], we already developed a preliminary model checker for tccp which uses constraints to achieve a compact representation of the system. Unfortunately, the expected state-explosion problem shows up when we combine the model with the property that we want to verify.

By considering the constraint system described in Section 2 for the tccp language, the tccp Structure which can be automatically obtained by following [9] only contains difference and stream constraints. Thus, in this work, our main idea is to represent that tccp Structure by means of a new symbolic structure (called DDD+LSs). Then, we extend to the new structure the existing efficient algorithms for manipulating DDDs [10] in order to verify tccp programs.

3.1   tccp *Structures* as Logic Formulas

A tccp *structure* can be translated into a formula of the logic underlying our constraint system similarly as it is done in the classical symbolic approach. The key idea is both to encode states by means of a logic formulae, and to represent the transition relation of the graph (i.e., the arcs of the graph) also with a logic formula which is defined from the labels of the nodes. Once we have the formula, we can construct a symbolic BDD-like structure corresponding to that formula, which represents an encoding of the system.

Let us explain how to obtain the formula by using the graph example shown in Figure 2. First, we can encode each arc as a conjunction of constraints. For example, the formula

$$\texttt{lget} \land \texttt{lask} \land \texttt{T1} \land \texttt{D1} \land \texttt{E1} \land \texttt{lt1}' \land \texttt{lt2}' \land \texttt{lbuild}' \land \texttt{lt}' \qquad (1)$$

represents the arc labelled with $a1$. In the following, we call *arc-formula* the logic formula representing an arc of the tccp structure. Note that we have used primed versions of agent labels to express their value in the following time instant.

Each arc of the graph corresponds to an element in the transition relation R. Then it is easy to see that the R relation can be represented by a disjunction of arc-formulas. The resulting formula is the input for the next task, where we symbolically represent it by means of the new structure (similar to BDDs). We define the algorithms that automatically construct such model from the formula.

3.2   The Symbolic Structure

In order to correctly represent tccp structures, we cannot directly use simple boolean structures such as BDDs, but the more sophisticated Difference Decision Diagrams (DDDs, [10]). The main reason for this is that nodes in DDDs may contain constraints (as states of the tccp structure) which can encode some implicit information whereas nodes in BDDs can contain only boolean variables.

DDDs are an extension of the BDDs to symbolically represent *difference constraint expressions*. Difference constraint expressions are formulas of a logic extended with difference constraints. Difference constraints are inequalities of the form $x - y \leq c$ where x and y are integer or real-valued variables, and c is a constant. A difference constraint expression consists of difference constraints combined with boolean connectives.

DDDs and BDDs share some common features. Both BDDs and DDDs can be ordered and reduced, and the algorithms to handle them are quite similar. A drawback of DDDs is that maintaining them as a canonical data structure is more expensive than for BDDs. Actually, if we reduce a DDD following the ideas of BDDs, then we do not obtain a canonical representation for the considered difference constraint expression, as opposed to the case of BDDs. However, it is still possible to obtain a semi-canonical[4] structure which can be used to decide satisfiability, validity, falsifiability and unsatisfiability of expressions.

Even though we can use DDDs to represent difference constraints, we need to model also constraints over streams (modeled as logical lists in tccp). Therefore, we need to extend the expressivity of DDDs and consistently redefine the algorithms which automatically construct the DDD Structure from a given formula.

Extending Difference Decision Diagrams with Logical Streams. Similarly to BDDs, *Difference Decision Diagrams + Logical Streams* (DDD+LSs) are directed acyclic graphs designed to handle the following logic:

$$\phi ::= x - y \leq c \mid \neg\phi \mid \phi_1 \wedge \phi_2 \mid \exists x.\phi \mid X = [x|Y] \mid X = [c|Y] \mid X = [\,]$$

where the constant c belongs to $\mathbb{D}$, and $X, Y \in \mathcal{V}$ denote variables. The grammar is extended as usually with the derived operators $x - y < c$, $\phi_1 \vee \phi_2$ and $\forall x.\phi$. Note that this logic is similar to the constraint system considered in this work. For the interested reader, a formal description of DDD+LSs is given in [1].

The key idea of this construction is that a node of a DDD+LS structure represents an expression which can be either a difference constraint or a stream constraint. Moreover, two arcs go out from each non-terminal node modeling the cases when the constraint represented by the node is satisfied or not. In Figure 3 (a), we show a DDD+LS structure representing the following formula.

$$\text{PD} - \text{PT} =< 4 \wedge \text{PT} - \text{PE} =< 7 \wedge \text{P} = [\text{PT} \mid \text{PT}_-] \tag{2}$$

In order to obtain an ordered graph structure which considers the new attributes of DDD+LS, we extend in the natural way the standard total order on the vertices of the graph defined in [10]. Intuitively, nodes containing difference expressions will appear in the graph structure before nodes containing stream expressions. The resulting formal definition of *Ordered* DDD+LS (called ODDD+LS in short) can be found in [1].

Following [10], we can consider semi-canonical structures to verify some properties. To get them, we apply some local and path reductions for ODDD+LSs, which are convenient extensions of the reductions defined for Ordered DDDs.

Roughly speaking, we first apply the local reduction which replaces constraints of the form $x < y$ by $x \leq y - 1$. Then, nodes which can be considered identical are eliminated, thus each node of the resulting Locally Reduced DDD+LS (LRDDD+LS) is different from the others.

The next step towards a suitable semi-canonical representation of DDD+LSs is the formulation of path reduction. The LRDDD+LS structure which results

---

[4] A DDD is semi-canonical if (i) an expression ϕ is represented by **1** iff ϕ is valid, and (ii) an expression ϕ is represented by **0** iff ϕ is unsatisfiable.

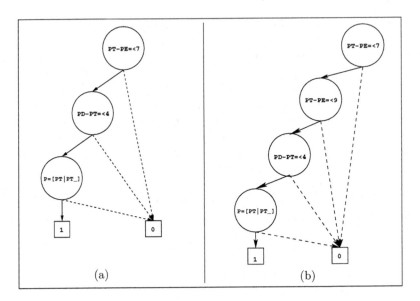

Fig. 3. Example: DDD+LS from the formula in (2)

from a path reduction step is called PRDDD+LS. Essentially, we can identify redundant arcs regarding difference constraint expressions by checking how expressions divide the domain. Each arc splits the domain into two disjoint subsets. If one of these subsets is empty, then we know that the arc is redundant.

In Figure 3 (b) we show a DDD+LS structure representing the formula in (2), which has a redundant node (the second one from the top). It is redundant since the part of the domain for which the constraint is not satisfied is empty. Thus we could eliminate it obtaining the DDD+LS shown in Figure 3 (a).

Theorem 1 below allows us to check properties in the PRDDD+LS in a safe way. We know that the expression represented by the node u is valid if and only if $u = 1$. If $u = 0$, then the expression is unsatisfiable. If u is a non terminal vertex, then we know that the expression is both satisfiable *and* falsifiable. The proof of this result can be found in [1].

Theorem 1 (semi-canonicity). *In a PRDDD+LS, the terminal vertex **1** is the only representation of valid expressions, and the terminal vertex **0** is the only representation of unsatisfiable expressions.*

4   Construction of DDD+LSs

In the present section, we provide the algorithms which automatically construct a LRDDD+LS structure from a given formula. From now, we assume that we are always considering LRDDD+LS. Vertices and arcs of the DDD+LS are stored in a graph data structure simply called *Graph*. Let G be a *Graph*. Initially, G

```
vertex MKD(G: graph, x ∈ V, y ∈ V, o: operator, c ∈ D, h: vertex, l: vertex)
    if D = Z ∧ o ='<' then c := c − 1; o :='≤'
    if member(G, (x, y, o, c, ⊥, ⊥, ⊥, h, l)) then
        return lookup(G, (x, y, o, c, ⊥, ⊥, ⊥, h, l))
    else if l = h then return l
        else if (x, y) = var(l) ∧ h = high(l) then return l
            else return insert(G, (x, y, o, c, ⊥, ⊥, ⊥, h, l))

vertex MKL(G: graph, x ∈ LV, y ∈ V, z ∈ LV, o: operator, h: vertex, l: vertex)
    if member(G, (⊥, ⊥, LIST, ⊥, x, y, z, h, l)) then
        return lookup(G, (⊥, ⊥, LIST, ⊥, x, y, z, h, l))
    else if l = h then return l
        else if (x, z) = var(l) ∧ h = high(l) then   return l
            else return insert(G, (⊥, ⊥, LIST, ⊥, x, y, z, h, l))
```

Fig. 4. Algorithms MKD and MKL that create vertices

contains only the two terminal vertices **0** and **1**. The set of arcs of G are implicitly stored via the attributes of its vertices.

Let us introduce some functions which allow us to access the information or modify the structure. First, the function insert(G, a) creates a new vertex v in G with attribute a, and returns v. The function member(G, a) returns true if there exists a vertex in graph G with attribute a. Finally, lookup(G, a) returns the vertex in G with attribute a.

In the following, we extend the algorithms defined in [10] for DDDs, to construct and handle the DDD+LS structures. We introduce some notation: $var(n)$ represents the variables of the constraint, and $high(n)$ $(low(n))$ represents the left-successor (right-successor) of node n.

In Figure 4, the algorithm MKD for difference constraints is given as a suitable extension of the algorithm presented in [10]. Also the algorithm MKL is presented which builds the vertex representing the stream expression $x=[y|z] \rightarrow h, l$.

The next step for the construction of the DDD+LS structure is to define the algorithms which combine difference and stream expressions with boolean operators. The idea is to recursively apply a specific operator to all the vertices in the DDD+LS Structure. In [5], this procedure is called APPLY. The same idea can be used for our DDD+LS structure.

We have called APPLS the corresponding algorithm for DDD+LSs. We show in Figure 5 this algorithm which follows closely the design of APPLY with some suitable adjustment to include the handling of the list expressions. In the pseudocode, 'Connective' denotes a boolean connective of the logic, whereas eval is a function which takes the two terminal vertices and a boolean connective as input and returns the truth value depending on the boolean connective. Additional notation is used in this algorithm: $op(n)$ tells us which kind of constraint the node represents, whereas $bound(n)$ states which kind of relation there exists between variables of the constraint. Moreover, *head*, *tail*, and *left* represent the different components of a list constraint.

Vertex APPLS(G: graph c: Connective, u: Vertex, v: Vertex)

r: Vertex

if $u, v \in \{0,1\}$ **then return** eval(c, u, v)

else if member($G, (c, u, v)$) **then return** lookup($G, (c, u, v)$)

   else if $var(u) < var(v)$ **then**

      if $op(u) =$ LIST **then** $r \leftarrow$ MKL($left(u), head(u), tail(u),$ APPLS($c, high(u), v$),
                                        APPLS($c, low(u), v$))

      else $r \leftarrow$ MKD($var(u), bnd(u),$ APPLS($c, high(u), v$), APPLS($c, low(u), v$))

      return r

   else if $var(u) = var(v)$ **then**

      if $bnd(u) < bnd(v) \wedge op(u) =$ LIST **then** $r \leftarrow$ MKL($left(u), head(u), tail(u),$
                                    APPLS($c, high(u), high(v)$), APPLS($c, low(u), v$))

      else if $bnd(u) < bnd(v) \wedge op(u) \neq$ LIST **then**
          $r \leftarrow$ MKD($var(u), bnd(u),$APPLS($c, high(u), high(v)$),APPLS($c, low(u), v$))

      else if $bnd(u) = bnd(v) \wedge op(u) =$ LIST **then** $r \leftarrow$ MKL($left(u), head(u), tail(u),$
                                  APPLS($c, high(u), high(v)$), APPLS($c, low(u), low(v)$))

      else if $bnd(u) = bnd(v) \wedge op(u) \neq$ LIST **then** $r \leftarrow$ MKD($var(u), bnd(u),$
                                  APPLS($c, high(u), high(v)$), APPLS($c, low(u), low(v)$))

      else if $bnd(u) > bnd(v) \wedge op(v) =$ LIST **then** $r \leftarrow$ MKL($left(v), head(v), tail(v),$
                                    APPLS($c, high(u), high(v)$), APPLS($c, u, low(v)$))

      else if $bnd(u) > bnd(v) \wedge op(v) \neq$ LIST **then**
          $r \leftarrow$ MKD($var(u), bnd(u),$ APPLS($c, high(u), high(v)$),APPLS($c, u, low(v)$))

   else if $var(u) > var(v)$ **then**

      if $op(u) =$ LIST **then** $r \leftarrow$ MKL($left(v), head(v), tail(v),$
                                  APPLS($c, u, high(v)$), APPLS($c, u, high(v)$))

      else $r \leftarrow$ MKD($var(v), bnd(v),$ APPLS($c, u, high(v)$), APPLS($c, u, high(v)$))

Fig. 5. Algorithm APPLS

5 Verification

In this section, we show how the symbolic structure can be used to formalize a symbolic model checking method for tccp programs. Assume that we express the property that we want to verify by using a CTL logic [6], where the atomic propositions of the logic are the same set of atomic propositions of the constraint system considered above. Note that we can use the corresponding entailment relation to obtain the truth value of formulas (see [4]).

We illustrate the method by an example. Assume that we want to verify that whatever state we check where the variables have been initialized, there exists a successor state where the same test succeeds. This property is expressed by the formula (3). We use the standard notation for temporal operators, thus $\mathbf{AG}(f)$ is the logic operator meaning that the formula f holds at each state in the future and $\mathbf{EX}(g)$ means that there exists a successor state where g is satisfied.

$$\mathbf{AG}(\neg \texttt{lask} \vee \mathbf{EX}(\texttt{lask})) \tag{3}$$

The classical symbolic model checking algorithm would take this formula as input and would return an OBDD representing the set of states of the system satisfying that formula. Temporal operators of the logic are represented as fixpoints [6] and then, symbolic structures are manipulated. In our approach we would substitute OBDDs by DDD+LSs and the CTL logic by the temporal logic of [4] which is interpreted over constraints.

[6] shows that is possible to associate a fix-point operator to each CTL formula which obtains the set of states starting from which the property holds. Since the formula $\mathbf{AG}(f)$ is equivalent to $f \wedge \mathbf{AX}(f)$, where $\mathbf{AX}$ means that the formula holds at each successive state, then it suffices to consider the operator associated to $f \wedge \mathbf{AX}(f)$. This operator allows us to compute a (greatest) fix-point which corresponds to the set of states starting from which the property to be proven holds. Finally if all initial states of the model (the tccp Structure) are included in the fix-point, then the formula is proven to hold in the system. In our example, the resulting algorithm proves that the formula holds.

6   Conclusions

We have generalized DDDs to a new structure which allows us to represent tccp programs symbolically. We have introduced the corresponding notions and algorithms for automatically construct the symbolic structures and we have shown how they can be used to formulate a lightweight, symbolic model checking algorithm. This novel symbolic methodology improves the automatic verification of reactive systems specified by using tccp as it reduces the search space significantly.

As future work, we plan to extend the language to consider constraint expressions more general than difference constraints. We also plan to complete and make publicly available a very cheap implementation of our method that we have already used for a preliminary evaluation of the methodology proposed in the paper over a small set of examples.

References

1. M. Alpuente, M. Falaschi, and A. Villanueva. Symbolic Representation Timed Concurrent Constraint Programs. Technical Report DSIC-II/12/04, DSIC, Technical University of Valencia, 2004. Available at www.dsic.upv.es/users/elp/villanue/papers/techrep04.ps.
2. M. Alpuente, M.M. Gallardo, E. Pimentel, and A. Villanueva. Abstract Model Checking of tccp programs. In *Proc. of the 2nd Workshop on Quantitative Aspects of Programming Languages (QAPL 2004)*, Electronic Notes in Theoretical Computer Science. Elsevier Science Publishers, 2004.
3. F. S. de Boer, M. Gabbrielli, and M. C. Meo. A Timed Concurrent Constraint Language. *Information and Computation*, 161:45–83, 2000.
4. F. S. de Boer, M. Gabbrielli, and M. C. Meo. A Temporal Logic for reasoning about Timed Concurrent Constraint Programs. In G. Smolka, editor, *Proc. of 8th International Symposium on Temporal Representation and Reasoning*, pages 227–233. IEEE Computer Society Press, 2001.

5. R. E. Bryant. Graph-based algorithms for Boolean function manipulation. *IEEE Transactions on Computers*, C-35(8):677–691, August 1986.
6. E. M. Clarke, O. Grumberg, and D. Peled. *Model Checking*. The MIT Press, Cambridge, MA, 1999.
7. E. M. Clarke, K. M. McMillan, S. Campos, and V. Hartonas-GarmHausen. Symbolic Model Checking. In *Proc. of the 8th International Conference on Computer Aided Verification*, volume 1102 of *Lecture Notes in Computer Science*, pages 419–422. Springer-Verlag, July/August 1996.
8. M. Falaschi, A. Policriti, and A. Villanueva. Modeling Timed Concurrent systems in a Temporal Concurrent Constraint language - I. In A. Dovier, M. C. Meo, and A. Omicini, editors, *Selected papers from 2000 Joint Conference on Declarative Programming*, volume 48 of *Electronic Notes in Theoretical Computer Science*. Elsevier Science Publishers, 2000.
9. M. Falaschi and A. Villanueva. Automatic verification of timed concurrent constraint programs. *Theory and Practice of Logic Programming*, 2004. To appear.
10. J. Møller, J. Lichtenberg, H.R. Andersen, and H. Hulgaard. Difference Decision Diagrams. In *Proc. of the 13th International Workshop on Computer Logic Science*, volume 1683 of *Lecture Notes in Computer Science*, pages 111–125, 1999.
11. V. A. Saraswat, M. Rinard, and P. Panangaden. Semantic Foundations of Concurrent Constraint Programming. In *Proc. of 18th Annual ACM Symposium on Principles of Programming Languages*, pages 333–352, New York, 1991. ACM Press.

A Methodology and a Framework for Model-Based Testing

Levi Lucio, Luis Pedro, and Didier Buchs

University of Geneva, Software Modelling and Verification Group,
24, Rue du Général Dufour,
CH-1211 Genève 4, Switzerland

Abstract. In this paper we will present a survey on the test case generation process and tools we are currently developing. It will reflect the new ideas that we're pursuing while keeping in mind our previous work on formal specification languages and theory of test case generation.

The model based test case generation method we propose is based on a subset of the Unified Modelling Language (UML) and the Object Constraint Language (OCL). It uses UML diagrams in what concerns the conceptual point of view and, in addition, OCL expressions for the system's behavioral description.

The research builds on past experience of the group while generating test cases starting from a model of the SUT (System Under Test) described in the *CO-OPN* formalism - formal language for system specification that acts as an intermediary format between the model and the tests.

Our method makes use of well known techniques such as symbolic execution by means of a logic resolution engine (i.e. Prolog) for state space exploration of the SUT.

1 Introduction

Testing has always been recognized as a fundamental part of the software development process. Despite, during long years testing was considered as an "annoying" task which often was done in an ad-hoc fashion. Nowadays, modern software development teams recognize the need for systematic testing in order to produce quality software. Unit-level testing tools allows to begin testing early in the process and motivates developers to think ahead to what tests they want to see running.

But, unit-level testing is usually performed at the class level and it only validates a specific unit of code. Since a system can be composed of many classes that agglomerate into subsystems, integration tests are also necessary. At the system level, these tests will reflect use cases that are pertinent and that exercise the system such that a certain level of confidence in it's reliability can be gained.

In order to build integration tests development teams usually follow certain protocols to achieve a good coverage of the SUT (System Under Test). These protocols are however often informal and the integration tests are built by hand

N. Guelfi (Ed.): RISE 2004, LNCS 3475, pp. 57–70, 2005.

according to the knowledge of the test engineer. This produces coverages of the SUT which are hardly qualifiable, much less quantifiable. The problem complexity grows exponentially with the size of the system.

On the other hand the theoretical field has already identified and sometimes solved many of the problems related to testing. See for example the work by Doong and Frankl in [2] or by Binder in [1]. However, the gap between theory and practice is still quite wide – only few tools for test case generation exist that make use of strong theories and are known/used in the software development arena. The goal of our research is to try to narrow this gap by wrapping the power of formal methods. In this paper we explain the methodology and the framework we are developing for test-case generation, which are fundamentally based on the work described in [3] by Gaudel and Marre and extended by us [7].

In order to make the description more pragmatic we have adopted a drink vending machine (DVM) example that we will use throughout the paper as an illustration of our approach.

The structure of the remaining text is as follows: first we'll provide the *Motivation and Principles* of our work; In second place, section *Modelling the Application*, defines model-base testing and we describe the modelling language that we are using; The next section, *Test Case Generation Machinery*, goes into the details and explains the process of generating test cases from a model of the SUT. We describe both the process and the tools that are already implemented or that we envisage for a near future; In *Application of Test Cases* we show how abstract test cases (sequences of operations) can be executed on a real application by means of a test driver.

2 Motivation and Principles

In a nutshell the goal of our work is to automate the generation of test cases as much as possible. To do that, we try to raise the level of abstraction at which humans have to intervene in the process. The idea is to capture the "intuition" of the tester about which aspects of the SUT should be tested, while leaving the job of translating those high-level intentions into concrete test cases to specialized machinery.

Since we use the model-based test case generation technique, an initial model of the application needs to be provided to the test case generation machinery. We have experience generating test cases from models expressed in the formal specification language *CO-OPN* (described by Biberstein, Buchs and Guelfi in [4]). However, since models of the SUTs have to be redone using *CO-OPN*, we found it difficult to apply to general software systems – concepts like abstract data types imply a construction of a new model for each SUT.

This said, we have decided to "wrap" our work using the Unified Modelling Language (UML) as the departure language for modelling the SUT – this will make our approach more general and easy to follow. Also, UML 2.0 includes OCL (Object Constraint Language) which allows more precise semantics than previous versions of this modelling language and enable us the possibility to use more than just constraints (where constrains stand for restriction on one or more values of an object oriented system) in order to better specify the system behavior - by means of OCL expressions in UML 2 it is possible, for example, to define queries.

Given a sufficiently expressive UML model of the SUT we then process it in order to generate test cases. The main problem with generating test cases for a software application is the fact that the exhaustive test set[1] is, in general, infinite. This is due to the fact that, for instance, a loop can be executed an infinite number of times or an input variable may have an infinite domain. We cope with this by introducing high-level test intentions, called *hypotheses*.

3   Modelling the Application

In this section we explain the concept of model test case generation. Furthermore, we discuss the *Fondue* [5] (object-oriented software development method that uses UML notations) modelling language we use to model the SUT and from were the test cases are generated.

3.1   Model-Based Test Case Generation

In model-based testing there are two main participants to the test process: the **specification model** and the **system under test (SUT)**. These two are connected by an *implementation relation* as shown in Fig. 1. For instance, based on the idea that the implementation has an observational behavior equivalent to the specification[7]. The idea behind it all is the following: in order to test a

Fig. 1. Model-based test case generation

SUT specification model of it must exist. Sequences of pairs *(operation,result)* are generated from the specification model. These sequences and respective outputs, which we call *test cases*, can then be applied to the SUT. If the SUT reacts to the stimuli in the same way the model did, the test case is successful. If not, the *implementation relation* cannot be established and the SUT does not conform to the model.

3.2   The Drink Vending Machine (DVM) Example

Throughout the paper we will often make reference to a drink vending machine (DVM) example as means of exemplifying our ideas. In the next lines we briefly state the DVM problem.

---

[1] Exhaustive meaning all the possible test cases over an SUT.

The controller for the DVM is supposed to coordinate the activities of the several components of the machine:

- *money box*: divided into two parts – the money collector that keeps the coins inserted to buy one drink; the money repository that holds all the coins gathered for selling drinks;
- *drink shelves*: there may exist several shelves, each one of them holding a particular kind of drink;
- *drink selection buttons*: one for each available drink type;
- *return coins button*: to abort a buy operation and return the already inserted coins;
- *display*: to display the amount of money already inserted.

A typical use case of the DVM would be the following: a client inserts a number of coins in the DVM and presses a drink selection button. The DVM distributes the chosen drink.

3.3   *Fondue* as Modelling Language

Since UML encompasses many different views over the same model, we have decided to restrict the number of these views we are effectively using. In particular, we have adopted the specification language of a methodology to specifying reactive system behavior. This approach called *Fondue* has been developed at the EPFL[5].

In terms of model specification, Fondue provides two main artifacts in order to describe the problem domain and the functional requirements of the system: *Concept* and *Behavior* Models. The first one is represented as *UML class diagrams* and defines the static structure of the system information. The *Behavior Model* defines the input and output communication of the system, and is divided in three models: *Environment, Protocol* and *Operation* - represented respectively by *UML collaboration diagrams, UML state diagrams* and *OCL operations*.

The following items provide a small description of each one of the Fondue Models illustrates them using the DVM example.

Environment Model: The environment model describes the interaction between the system and its environment. All possible inputs and outputs of the system are made explicit. Figure 2 depicts the environment model for the DVM.

Concept Model: To define the system's state the *Fondue* approach uses the Concept Model. This model allows the expression of concepts of the problem's domain in terms of *classes* and *associations*. The populations of instances of those classes and associations define the system's state at a given moment. Figure 3 shows the concept model for the DVM.

Protocol Model: With the Protocol model it is possible to specify the dynamic behavior of the system over logical time. This model is expressed by means of

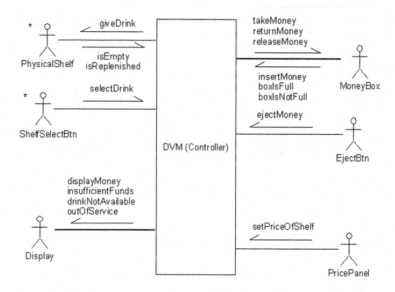

Fig. 2. Environment model for the DVM

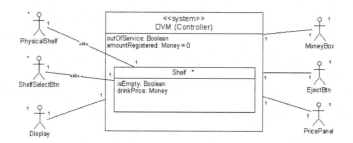

Fig. 3. Concept model for the DVM

state machines which capture the way the system responds to requests depending on its current state.

Operation Model: The Operation model defines the requests that the system is able to answer and how these effect on the system's state. Besides defining the parameters of an operation, this model defines its pre- and post-condition. The pre-condition describes assumptions about the state of the system before the operation is executed. The post-condition describes how the state of the system evolves after the operation is executed and which output messages are produced. The next example describes an operation for the DVM:

```
Operation: DVM::insertMoney (m: Money);
Description:
Use Cases: buy drink;
Aliases:
```

```
Messages: Display::{DisplayMoney; DrinkNotAvailable; InsufficientFunds};
          MoneyBox::{ReleaseMoney;};
Pre:
Post:
    self.display^drinkNotAvailable(false) &
    self.display^insufficientFunds(false) &
    if not self.outOfService then -- condition
                                        ensures that money box is not full.
        self.amountRegistered = self.amountRegistered@pre + m &
        3self.display^displayMoney(self.amountRegistered)
    else
          self.moneyBox^releaseMoney()
    endif;
```

4   Test Case Generation Machinery

In this section we will describe our approach to the generation of test cases from a *Fondue* model. We start by giving an overview picture of the process we are putting in place and in a second phase we focus on each of the individual parts of that process.

We can define *Test Case* as a pair composed of a sequence of requests on the SUT/expected outputs, and a verdict. The verdict belongs to the set {*true, false*} and reflects the validity of the sequence of requests against the expected behavior of the SUT, as defined in the specification.

This definition allow us to search for test cases that should be both accepted and not accepted by the SUT. The implementation relation requires strict respect of the model behavior.

4.1   The Test Case Generation Framework

The activity of test case generation can be seen as the process of finding a set of test cases which is pertinent and finite. Pertinence means that: the test set will discard a SUT if it does not fulfill the expectations; the test set will never reject a correct SUT.

Having in mind that the application under test may allow infinite sequences of events or an input value may belong to an infinite domain, the process we are putting in place needs to provide the tools to reduce the initial test set to a finite one that is pertinent.

In Fig. 4 we depict the full picture of the process of test case generation we are investigating. In the figure the arrows represent activities and the ellipses/circles represent artifacts involved in the process. The process is divided in two different parts: the left side of the figure represents the test case generation process; the right side, their application, results and the various components that are used. In this subsection we will focus on the part of the process that concerns how the tests are generated - this means that all references to Fig. 4 are related to its left side.

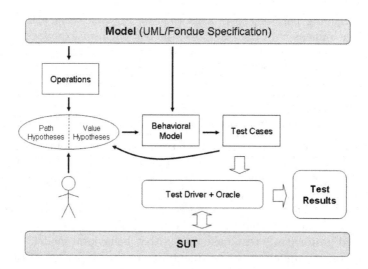

Fig. 4. Test Case generation process

The bent arrow coming from the the Model denote the activities of deriving from the specification: the *signatures*[2] of the possible operations over the SUT and a *behavioral model* of the SUT. During the test case generation process the operation signatures are organized in sequences that form the test cases. On the other hand, it becomes necessary to validate those sequences, i.e. to find the verdict for the test case. The *behavioral model* is an executable model derived from the specification that allows the automatic manipulation of an abstract state space of the SUT.

The process we describe in Fig. 4 is not fully automatic. The bottom left matchstick man represents human interactions while providing heuristics that reduce the initial infinite test set. These heuristics are provided as hypotheses over the shape of the test cases to be generated. These hypotheses are based on temporal logic formulas that allow us to express test intentions for COOPN specifications. The input/output pairs mentioned earlier in this paper, are expressed by the temporal logic formulas which are the main basis of the test/constraint language that is under development by our group. In general, we encapsulate the temporal logic using a language of constraints and the graphs of input/output pairs that they represent correspond to: operations performed on the system - input; observable results of the operations - outputs. The hypotheses (bottom bent arrow in the figure) may be provided either as patterns over the sequence of operations – path hypotheses; or as constraints over the parameters of those operations – value hypotheses.

---

[2] The signature of an operation is composed of the operation name and the name and type of each of the operation's parameters.

The remaining part of the process that we are analyzing has to do with the iterative refinement of the test cases: the test engineer expresses hypotheses about the functioning of the SUT that narrow the initial infinite test set. If the produced test set is not yet the expected one, another more refined iteration of the process is done.

4.2   Deriving the Behavioral Model

The behavioral model is the component that allows the automatic exploration of the state space derivable from the specification of the SUT. However, the step of turning a *Fondue* model into a sort of high level prototype of the final application is not trivial.

We split our test case generation research project in two main areas: **model treatment** – meaning extracting from the *Fondue* model a functional behavioral model – and **generating test cases** using that behavioral model. In between, we have an *intermediate format*: representation of the SUT using *CO-OPN*. The reason why we have chosen *CO-OPN* is the fact that we have already a translator that transforms it into Prolog. The Prolog result of this transformation can then be used to explore operationally the behavior of the specification. This means that the UML model has to be interpreted into a *CO-OPN* specification and that the test case generation engine will pickup from there. We have built a Prolog runtime engine (described by Buffo and Buchs in [6]) *CO-OPN* that allows us to manipulate automatically the state space produced by the UML specification.

The runtime engine is able to simulate the evolution in the state space of the model as operations are applied to it. In fact, we are able to represent in Prolog both the model itself – in the *CO-OPN* – and the state space produced by it. Since *Fondue* is an object-oriented approach, the runtime engine has to know how to deal with such concepts as: object management, polymorphism, navigation through associations between classes and concurrency[3]. The next example shows (a part of) the concept diagram of the DVM (in Fig. 3) in our intermediate format:

```
Class DVMController;
Interface
    Methods
        put _ outOfService : Boolean;
        get _ amountRegistered : Money;
Body
    Places
        outOfService : Boolean;
        amountRegistered : Money = 0;
End DVMController;
```

---

[3] The work on concurrency is inspired by our research on expressing the operational semantics of *CO-OPN*.

```
Class DMVShelf;
Interface
    Methods
        isEmpty : Boolean;
        drinkPrice : Money;
End DMVShelf;

Class ControllerShelfAssociation;
Morphism
    DVMControllerInstance -> DVMShelfInstalce;
End ControllerShelfAssociation;
```

The two classes in the system – DVM and Shelf – are defined as well as the composition association between them.

The behavior of the Fondue operations is translated into pre- and post conditions of the intermediate format. Meta rules defined in the runtime kernel provides rules for: embedding local states of each pre and post condition into the whole object system; managing the synchronizations between sub-systems; compute concurrent behaviors as well as sequence of operations. These meta-rules are inspired by the transactional and concurrent semantics of the *CO-OPN* formalism. In the future we expect to be able to deal, using all *CO-OPN* features, with composition of Fondue subsystems and with concurrency related behaviors. A *pre* or *post* condition has the form *IFprepost(event,pre,post)* :- *body* where:

event = with(operation,emitted events) is the behaviour of the operation *operation* described for a given structure of events emitted (*emited events*). The emitted events can be structured with sequential, non-determinism and simultaneity operators. Creation operators can also be included into this event structure;

pre and post describe the states before and after the operation occurs.

body is a collection of constraint that must be fulfilled by the variables that can appear into the *event*, *pre* and *post* expressions.

We use the runtime engine to: verify whether a concrete test case (in other words, an execution trace) exists[4] in the state space of the model; find test cases that obey to certain criteria (e.g. if the criteria is *true*, then Prolog would return all successful test cases, meaning all the possible execution traces of the specification).

Although the runtime engine for the intermediate format already exists and the intermediate format itself is nearly stable, all the interpretation machinery that will convert the *Fondue* model into a *CO-OPN* model is under development. We are counting on doing this by expressing the model in a tool for representing UML/Fondue diagrams[5]. The tool provides the functionality that allow us to export the diagrams using the XML Meta Data Interchange (XMI). This XMI

---

[4] Prolog replies *yes* or *no* depending on whether the test case is executable or not.

[5] Any CASE tool that could provide the possibility to endorse a Fondue Module can be used. For the moment, we're using a module of Fondue for Together (http://www.borland.com/together/).

can then be loaded by any implementation of the Meta Data Repository (MDR) and the navigation within the exported model is enabled by means of Java Metadata Interface (JMI). A set of well defined transformation rules provide the functionality to map a Fondue model into a COOPN one. This part of the work is being developed at the time that this paper is being written and the general approach is to use Model Driven Architecture (MDA) technics and Meta-Model levels both to concretize a transformation definitions between the two models. It is also our objective to use standard approaches to implement a transformation tool that will allow to systematize and automatize this part of the Test Generation framework.

4.3   Applying Hypotheses

To express the heuristics that help excluding from the final test set the ones that aren't relevant, we have defined a language to express *hypotheses* about the functioning of the SUT. The rationale behind the approach is that the stronger the hypotheses, the more important the reduction in the exhaustive test set. We have built a theory[7] behind the concept of applying hypotheses that reduce the exhaustive test set without losing pertinence.

As was previously mentioned in the paper and shown in Fig. 4 there are two main variables over which it is possible to express hypotheses: *paths*, meaning the form of the sequences of operations; *values*, meaning the parameters of those operations. In what concerns *paths*, the hypotheses are given by regular expressions that allow the definition of sequences of operations. The language makes use of the operators: $*$ for zero or more repetitions; $+$ and one or more repetitions; AND and OR for connecting sequences of operations. For convenience we have also defined a *lowerT* operator that bounds the upper limit of repetitions of an operation. As an example assume we have operations x and y in our SUT. With the hypotheses $x*y$ OR x, possible test cases would be yx, xy or $xxxyx$. In what concerns *values*, we can apply two types of hypotheses:

Uniformity: if a test case containing a variable v is valid for one value of v, then it is valid for all of v's domain. This type of hypotheses can be compared to random testing;

Regularity: if a test case containing a variable v is valid for a subdomain of v satisfying a given complexity criteria, then it is valid for all of v's subdomains of greater complexity.

Uniformity hypotheses can be seen as a particular case of the regularity hypotheses where the subdomain under test only contains one element.

The next example shows a Prolog goal that calculates a test set for the DVM:

```
//THIS SHOULD ALSO BE CHANGED BY AN EXAMPLE USING THE CONSTRAINTS
(Levi's NEW IDEAS)

solve([pattern(_,and(star(ev(insertMoney(1),_),N),ev(selectDrink(S),_)),L),
lowerT(nat,N,5)]),uniform(L),valid(L,true).
```

The goal can be splited into three parts:

1. prefixed by the predicate *solve*[6] states an hypotheses over the *path* that reduces the focus to sequences of five *insertMoney* operations followed by one *selectDrink* operation[7];
2. prefixed by the predicate *uniform* chooses randomly one value for all the variables that remain uninstantiated in the test set. In this case the only uninstantiated variable is the type of drink (denoted by S).
3. prefixed by the predicate *valid* validates the previously obtained test sets against the behavioral model in order to find their verdict. In this case we are only interested in tests that are accepted stated here by the *true* parameter.

Since the mechanism for automatically generating the behavioral model is not implemented, we have coded by hand a behavioral model of the DVM. This allowed us to run the Prolog goal stated above and to obtain the test set:

```
with(selectDrink(Water),[insufficientFunds])
with(insertMoney(1),[]), with(selectDrink(Fanta),[insufficientFunds])
with(insertMoney(1),[]), with(insertMoney(1),[]), with(selectDrink(Fanta),
   [giveDrink(Fanta)])
```

In fact, five test cases are generated by the engine but due to their size we only present three. It is possible to see that the mechanism generates sequences of operations along with their expected outputs.

4.4   Subdomain Decomposition

While discussing the application of *uniformity hypotheses* we mentioned that it can be compared to random testing. In fact, applying uniformity over a variable with a given domain will yield a single value from that domain, picked at chance. Although this hypotheses is useful, it can be refined.

Consider for example that in the application of the hypotheses in Sec. 4.3, Pag. 67, we have not a sequence of *insertMoney(1)* operations but rather one single *insertMoney(N)* operation – where N represents the number of coins to insert – followed by the *selectDrink(S)* one. In this case, a uniformity hypotheses applied over N and S would produce one single test case with N and S instantiated to random values. The interest of this test set is arguable.

To improve the situation, one can reason about the interesting values that N can assume. There are three situations that can be induced by values of N:

− if $N \in \{0, .., price\,of\,drink\,S - 1\}$ drink S is not distributed;
− if $N \in \{price\,of\,drink\,S\}$ drink S is distributed;
− if $N \in \{price\,of\,drink\,S + 1..\infty\}$ drink S is distributed and the excess money is given back to the client;

---

[6] The *solve* predicate is related to the fact that we have substituted Prolog's SLD by another resolution mechanism to better fit our needs.

[7] In our Prolog representation, the $*$ operator is expressed by the predicate *star* and the $+$ operator by the predicate *plus*.

Ideally, a uniformity hypotheses over N would produce not only one but three values, corresponding to each one of the three situations stated above. This can be done by searching the behavioral model of the specification symbolically in the sense that the points of decision are explored for both *true* and *false* conditions. At the end of this exploration, each possible execution path will be represented by a set of constraints on variables (operation parameters) produced by the accumulation of conditions at each of the points of decision. The final step will be to instantiate the variables participating in the set of constraints that denotes each execution path. The implementation of this mechanism is done in Prolog with resolution stopping at the decision points.

5   Application of Test Cases

Finally, it is necessary to apply to the SUT the tests produced by the process described in the previous section. In Fig. 4 this step is expressed on the right side of the picture. As can be seen, a piece of machinery called the *test driver* is needed in order to apply the sequence of operations to the SUT must to observe if the outputs correspond to the expected ones. The top matchstick man acts as an intermediary between the Model, SUT interface and the test driver. The signatures of the operations are derived from the Model and, since there is a relation of 1 to 1 between the specification and the SUT connect, we can then interface the *test driver* to the SUT interface by means of mapping rules.

Coupled with the test driver is the *oracle*, which is a decision procedure that decides whether a test case should pass or fail. The user (bottom matchstick man) provides observation hypotheses that will be used by the *oracle* to decide wether the test is accepted or not. A test case accepted by the model should be accepted by the SUT and vice-versa for one that is not accepted. If this is the case the SUT passes the test, otherwise an error is detected.

We have implemented a very simple DVM on the web that allows all the main interactions described by the problem statement in Sect. 3.2. The user is capable of (virtually) buying a drink by clicking on an *insert money* link a number of times and then clicking a link corresponding to name of the drink to choose it. We have put online two DVMs, one functioning correctly and one that takes the money but does not distribute the drink.

In order to find the error we applied the test cases that were found in Sect. 4.3. To apply the tests we have used a trial version of a tool called Astra QuickTest^{TM}. The tool provides facilities to test web pages by providing unitary actions that can be assembled into test cases. A small translator script was written to pass from the abstract test case format (see **??**) to the language of Astra QuickTest^{TM}. An example of a test case translated into the driver's language is shown in the following lines:

```
Browser("The Drink Vending").Page("The Drink Vending").Link("Reset DVM").Click
Browser("The Drink Vending").Page("The Drink Vending").Link("Insert 1 coin").Cli
Browser("The Drink Vending").Page("The Drink Vending").Link("Insert 1 coin").Cli
```

```
Browser("The Drink Vending").Page("The Drink Vending").Link("Choose 1 Fanta").Cli
Browser("The Drink Vending").Page("The Drink Vending").Check CheckPoint("Heres yo
```

In this specific case the test driver tool is coupled with the *oracle* since Astra QuickTest^{TM} decides automatically whether a test case passes or not.

6   Related Work

A large number of papers on model-based test case generation exists in the literature. However, not many deal with models expressed in semi-formal languages such as UML.

At the university of Franche-Comté an approach to test case generation similar to ours is being developed. Legeard and Peureux explain in [8] their method which consists in: translating a UML specification into a program in an adapted logic programming language similar to Prolog; explore symbolically the state space of the model searching for values for parameters of operations that are interesting to test. The procedure is an evolution of what we described in Sect. 4.4.

Pretschner et al explain in [9] their approach which starts from a model described in AUTOFOCUS^{TM}, a tool based on UML-RT (for Real-Time systems). The framework also makes use of a logic programming language to explore symbolically the state space.

7   Future Work

This paper describes work that is in progress. In the agenda for the next steps the coding of the algorithms that will translate a *Fondue* model into the *CO-OPN* and the operational implementation of full sub-domain decomposition. At the same time we are re-evaluating our hypotheses language with the goal of specializing it – a catalog of domain-dependent hypotheses is something we are looking into – and also to develop a graphical user interface for the expression of hypotheses based in a formalized test/constraint language.

References

1. Binder, R. V.: Testing object-oriented software: a survey. Journal of Testing, Verification and Reliability, 6:125252, 1996.
2. Doong, R.-K. and Frankl, P. G.: The ASTOOT approach to testing object-oriented programs. ACM Transactions on Software Engineering and Methodology, 3(2):101130, 1994.
3. Bernot, G., Gaudel, M.-C., and Marre, B.: Software testing based on formal specifications: a theory and a tool. IEEE Software Engineering Journal, 6(6):387405, 1991.
4. Biberstein, O., Buchs, D. and Guelfi, N.: Object-oriented nets with algebraic specifications: The *CO-OPN/2* formalism. In G. Agha and F. De Cindio, editors, *Advances in Petri Nets on Object-Orientation*, Lecture Notes in Computer Science. Springer-Verlag, 1998.

5. Strohmeier, A.: Fondue: An Object-Oriented Development Method based on the UML Notation. In X Jornada Técnica de Ada-Spain, Documentación, Lunes 12 de Noviembre 2001, ETSI de Telecommunicación, Universidad Politécnica de Madrid, Madrid, Spain, November 2001.
6. Buffo, M. and Buchs, D.: Symbolic simulation of coordinated algebraic petri nets using logic programming. To be published: internal note, University of Geneva, 2004.
7. Péraire, C., Barbey, S. and Buchs D.: Test selection for object-oriented software based on formal specifications. In Proc. of Programming Concepts and Methods (PROCOMET) 98, pages 385-403, 1998.
8. Legeard, B. and Peureux, F.: Génération de séquences de tests à partir d'une spécification B en PLC ensembliste. In Proc. Approches Formelles dans l'Assistance au Développement de Logiciels, pages 113-130, June 2001.
9. Pretschner, A. et al: Model-based test case generation for smart cards. In Proc. Formal Methods for Industria Critical Systems, 2003.

An Exception Monitoring System for Java*

Heejung Ohe and Byeong-Mo Chang

Department of Computer Science,
Sookmyung Women's University,
Seoul 140-742, Korea
{lutino, chang}@sookmyung.ac.kr

Abstract. Exception mechanism is important for the development of robust programs to make sure that exceptions are handled appropriately at run-time. In this paper, we develop a dynamic exception monitoring system, which can trace handling and propagation of thrown exceptions in real-time. With this tool, programmers can examine exception handling process in more details and handle exceptions more effectively. Programmers can also trace only interesting exceptions by selecting options before execution. It can also provides profile information after execution, which summarizes exception handling in each method during execution. To reduce performance overhead, we implement the system based on code inlining, and presents some experimental results.

Keywords: Java, exception propagation, exception analysis.

1 Introduction

Exception handling is important in modern software development because it can support the development of robust programs with reliable error detection, and fast error handling. Java provides facilities to allow the programmer to define, throw and catch exceptional conditions. Because uncaught exceptions will abort the program's execution, it is important for the development of robust programs to make sure that exceptions are handled appropriately at run-time. However, it is not easy for programmers to trace and handle exceptions effectively.

A number of static exception analyses including our previous works have been proposed based on static analysis framework [2, 3, 9, 10]. They approximate all possible exceptions, and don't consider unchecked exceptions usually. The static analysis information is usually used to check that all uncaught (checked) exceptions are specified in the method header. They, however, are not able to provide exact information on how exceptions are thrown, caught and propagated at runtime.

To assist developing robust software, we need a tool to trace or monitor raised exceptions effectively during execution. For example, J2ME Wireless Tool

---

* This Research was supported by the Sookmyung Women's University Research Grants 2004.

N. Guelfi (Ed.): RISE 2004, LNCS 3475, pp. 71–81, 2005.

Kit(WTK), a dynamic analysis tool, provides just the names of exceptions, whenever exceptions are thrown, but it cannot trace how thrown exceptions are handled and propagated. In addition, J2ME WTK is too slow when tracing exceptions, because it relies on JVMPI. Programmers cannot trace propagation and handling of exceptions with this tool. To develop reliable and robust Java programs, programmers need a more powerful tool, which can trace exception propagation and exception handling during execution.

In this paper, we develop a dynamic exception monitoring system, which can trace how thrown exceptions(including unchecked exceptions) are handled and propagated in real-time. Programmers can examine exception handling process in more details and handle exceptions more effectively. Moreover, programmers can trace only interesting exceptions by selecting options before execution. It also provides profile information after execution, which summarizes exception handling in each method during execution.

To reduce performance overhead, we design the system based on code inlining. Input programs are transformed by inlining codes so as to trace only interesting exceptions according to user options. The transformed programs produce trace information during execution, and profile information after execution. We implement the event monitoring system in Java based on Barat [1], which is a front-end for a Java compiler. We also present some experimental results, which can show the effectiveness of the system.

The rest of this paper is organized as follows. The next section gives preliminaries on exceptions. Section 3 describes overall design of the system. Section 4 describes the implementation of the system, and Section 5 presents some experiments. Section 6 concludes this paper and discusses further research topics.

2   Preliminaries

Like normal objects, exceptions can be defined by classes, instantiated, assigned to variables, passed as parameters, etc. Exception facilities in Java allow the programmer to define, throw and catch exceptional conditions. The throw statement throw e_0 evaluates e_0 first, and then throws the exception object. The try statement try S_1 catch $(c \ x) \ S_2$ evaluates S_1 first. If the statement S_1 executes normally without thrown exception, the try-catch statement executes normally. If an exception is thrown from S_1 and its class is covered by c then the handler expression S_2 is evaluated with the exception object bound to x. If the thrown exception is not covered by class c then the thrown exception continues to propagate back along the call chain until it meets another handler. The programmers have to declare in a method definition any exception class whose exceptions may escape from its body. The formal semantics of Java was proposed in [5] with exception throwing, propagation and handling taken into consideration.

Let's consider a simple example in Figure 1, which shows exception propagation. The thrown exception E1 from the method m2 is propagated through m2 and m1, and caught by the try-catch in the main method. The exception

```
class Demo{
  public static void main(String[] args ) throws E2
  {
     try {
         m1( );
     } catch (E1 x) {  ; }
     . . .
     m3( );
  }

  void m1( ) throws E1{
     m2( );
  }

  void m2( ) throws E1{
     if (...) throw new E1();
  }

  void m3( ) throws E2 {
     if (...) throw new E2();
     if (...) m3( );
  }
}
```

Fig. 1. An example program for exception propagation

E2 may be thrown from the method m3. If it is thrown, then it is propagated until the **main** method and not caught. The method m3 also has a recursive call to itself, so that the thrown exception E2 may be propagated back through the recursive calls.

Because uncaught exceptions will abort the program's execution, it is important for the development of robust programs to check that exceptions are handled appropriately at run-time.

3 Design Considerations

There are several ways that monitors can mediate all application operations. A traditional reference monitor is implemented by halting execution before certain machine instructions and invoking the reference monitor with the instruction as input. An alternate implementation, not limited by hardware support, runs applications inside an interpreter like JVM that executes the application code and invokes a reference monitor before each instruction. JVMPI(JVM Profiler Interface) follows this approach. However, this approach has unacceptable performance overhead [6], since a cost is incurred on every executed instruction. The third option inlines reference monitors in the target software. This approach is shown to overcome the limitations of traditional reference monitors, yet exhibits reasonable performance [6].

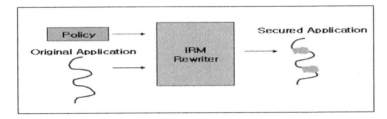

Fig. 2. Inlined monitor [6]

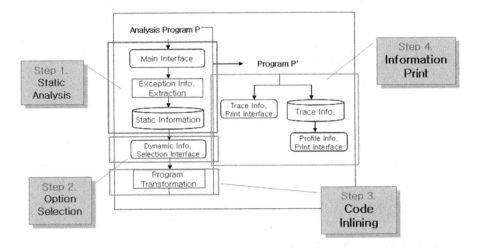

Fig. 3. System architecture

An inlined reference monitor is obtained by modifying an application to include the functionality of a reference monitor. As in Figure 2, IRMs are inserted into applications by a rewriter or transformer that reads a target application and a policy, and produces a secured application, whose execution monitors its execution. The inlining approach is shown to be efficient for monitoring Java programs in [6].

We follow the inlining approach to design a dynamic exception monitoring system for efficiency. We take the following things into consideration in the design.

The first one is to provide users with options to select interesting exceptions. By selecting options before execution, users can focus on interesting exceptions and methods by tracing only interesting exceptions in real-time. This option can also contribute in reducing performance overhead, because it makes the system to trace only interesting exceptions instead of all exceptions. The second one is to provide a profile option to produce profile information after execution, which summarizes exception throwing and handling during execution. The third one is to reduce performance overhead. We try to reduce performance overhead by inlining code instead of using JVMPI. An input program P is transformed into a program P' by inlinig codes so as to trace only interesting exceptions according to user options. The transformed program P' will trace how thrown exceptions are handled and propagated during execution, and give profile information on exception handling after execution.

Overall architecture of the system is shown in Figure 3. This system consists of four steps as in Figure 3. The function of each step is as follows:

The first step extracts exception-related constructs by static analysis. This static information is used to give users options. The second step is option selection, where users can select interesting exceptions and methods using the static exception information. Users can trace only interesting exceptions and methods by selecting options in this step. The third step is a transformer, which transforms an input program P into a program P' by inlining codes so as to trace only interesting exceptions according to user options. The fourth step is to compile and execute the transformed program P'. It is to be executed on Java 2 SDK or J2ME WTK.

4   Implementation

The exception monitoring system is implemented in Java based on Barat [1], which is a front-end for a Java compiler. Barat builds an abstract syntax tree for an input Java program and enriches it with type and name analysis information. It also provides interfaces for traversing abstract syntax trees, based on visitor design pattern in [7]. We can traverse AST nodes and do some actions or operations at visiting each node using a visitor, which is a tree traverse routine based on design patterns. Barat provides several visitors as basic visitors: `DescendingVisitor` which traverses every AST node in depth-first order and `OuputVisitor` which outputs input programs by traversing AST nodes. We can develop a static analyzer by implementing visitors to do necessary actions or operations at visiting AST nodes by extending basic visitors [1].

As described in Figure 3, our system consists of four steps. We implement the first three steps. The last step is a real execution on Java SDK.

A main window for selecting options is shown in Figure 5, which shows all files in the package of a benchmark program *Check* from specjvm98. After users select files from the package, the window displays a list of exceptions, handlers and methods based on the static analysis information. Then, users can select only interesting exceptions, handlers and methods among them. By selecting options, users can get only interesting trace information and focus on interesting exceptions when debugging.

Fig. 4. Architecture of Barat

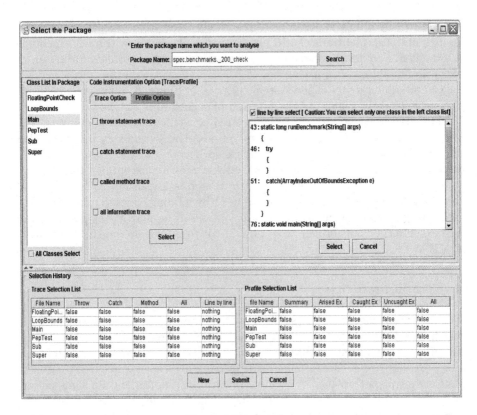

Fig. 5. Menu window

```
Class TransformVisitor extends OutputVisitor{
    visitThrow{
    // Print the location of thrown exception and its type
    }
    visitTry{
    // Print the location of try statement
    }
    visitCatch{
    // Print the location of catch statement, the type of caught exception
    // call printStackTrace() method
    }
    visitMethod{
    // Print the method information and record exception propagation
    // via this method
    }
}
```

Fig. 6. Structure of TransformVisitor

```
28   synchronized int syncMethod2(int y) throws ArithmeticException {
29
30      pi.print_methodtrace("syncTest","syncMethod2","27","synchronized null syncMethod2(int y) throws Arithme
31      pi.methodcollect("syncTest","syncMethod2","|ArithmeticException|");
32      this.x = this.x + y;
33
34      if (this.x == 99){
35          pi.print_throwtrace("syncTest","syncMethod2","30","new ArithmeticException");
36          pi.set_ThrowInfo("syncTest" , "syncMethod2" , "30" ,"new ArithmeticException");
37          throw (new ArithmeticException("fisk"));
38      }
39
40      return this.x;
41   }
42
43   public static void main(String[] args) {
44       try{
45
46          pi.print_methodtrace("syncTest","main","34","static void main(String[] args)");
47          pi.methodcollect("syncTest","main","|");
48      syncTest sy = new syncTest();
49      int xx = sy.syncMethod(4);
50      xx = sy.syncMethod2(4);
51          }catch(Exception apple)  {
52              apple.printStackTrace();
53          }
54          finally{
55              pi.print_Profile();
56          }
57   }
```

Fig. 7. Transformed program

To provide users with options, we implement a static analyzer to extract exception-related constructs by extending `DescendingVisitor`. It extracts static information about possible exceptions and methods by analyzing input programs statically. In particular, it extracts static program constructs on exception raising, handling and methods.

We implement a program transformer called `TransformVisitor` by extending `OuputVisitor`, which transforms an input program P into a program P' by inlining codes so as to trace handling and propagation of thrown exceptions according to selected options. Figure 6 shows overall structure of the program transformer.

A fragment of the transformed `Check` program is displayed in Figure 7. This figure shows `main` method and `syncMethod2` which is called from the main method. The codes in the box are inlined codes by the transformer. The transformed program is to be executed automatically in Java 2 SDK. This transformed code traces how thrown exceptions are handled and propagated in real-time during execution. In addition, it can also profile exception handling of each method during execution and shows the number of thrown, caught, and uncaught exceptions for each method after execution.

5   Experiments

We have implemented the system with SDK 1.4.2 on Pentium 4 processor and Window XP. We first tested it with *Check* from specjvm98, which is a program to check that the JVM fits the requirements of the benchmark.

When we execute the transformed program, we can trace handling and propagation of thrown exceptions (including runtime exceptions) as in Figure 8. It shows the location and exception type when an exception is thrown. It also shows the propagated path when an propagated exception is caught by a `catch`-clause. For example, the propagation path of `ArithmeticException`, when it is caught at line 659, is shown in Figure 8 When the program terminates, it profiles the thrown, caught, and propagated exceptions of each method. Figure 9 shows the names and numbers of thrown, caught and propagated exceptions of each method. It also shows the name of exceptions, which is specified by `throws` clause at method headers. For example, `ArithmeticException` is specified at `PepTest.syncMethod2`.

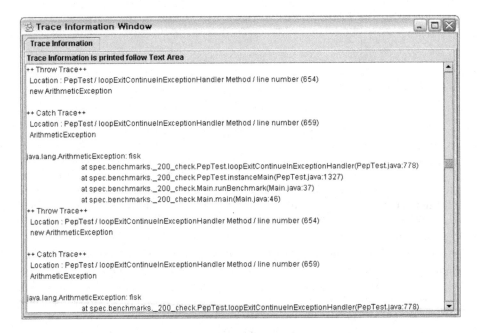

Fig. 8. Trace of Check program

We have experimented the system with five Java benchmark programs. The first one is the small server connecting program *ServerStuff*. The second one is *Linpack* benchmark, which is to solve a dense system of linear equations. The third one is *Check* from specjvm98. The fourth one is *Jess* from specjvm98, which is an expert system shell based on NASA's CLIPS program. The last one is *Rex* from gnu, which matches a regular expression against strings.

Table 1 first shows the numbers of lines of benchmark programs before and after inlining, and then shows the number of thrown exceptions, the number of caught exceptions, and the number of propagated exceptions for each benchmark. If an exception is propagated, it is counted as propagated exceptions at every

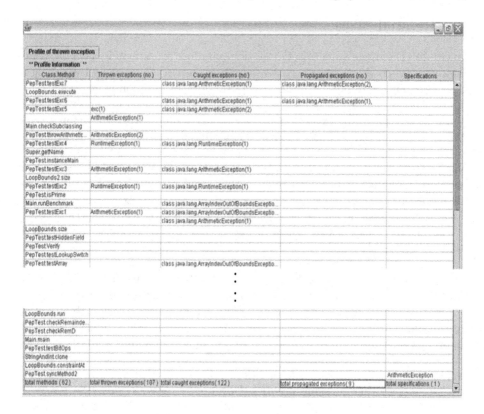

Fig. 9. Profile of Check program

Table 1. Experiments with benchmark programs

Programs	Lines(before)	Lines(after)	Throw	Caught	Propagated
ServerStuff	71	104	2	2	4
Linpack	1057	1103	1	1	17
Check	1817	1898	107	122	9
Jess	542	574	1	1	10
Rex	3198	3308	1	1	6

method, through which it is propagated back. So a propagated exception can be counted multiply.

The listed figures of *Jess* represents propagation of a thrown exception when an input with wrong syntax is given. The listed figures of *Rex* also represents propagation of a thrown exception when a wrong option is given. The listed figures of *Check* represents the many numbers of thrown, handled and propagated exceptions.

6   Related Works

In [10, 11], the usage patterns of exception-handling constructs in Java programs were studied to show that exception-handling constructs are used frequently in Java programs and more accurate exception flow information is necessary.

Exception analyses have been studied actively based on static analysis framework [2, 3, 12, 9]. Static exception analyses analyze input programs before execution and provide approximate information about all possible uncaught exceptions of each method. In Java[8], the JDK compiler ensures, by an intraprocedural analysis, that clients of a method either handle the exceptions declared by that method, or explicitly specify them at method header. In [9], a tool called Jex was developed to analyze uncaught exceptions in Java. It can extract the uncaught exceptions in Java programs, and generate views of the exception structure.

In our previous work [2, 12], we proposed interprocedural exception analysis that estimates uncaught exceptions independently of programmers's specified exceptions. We compared our analysis with JDK-style analysis by experiments on realistic Java programs. We also have shown that our analysis can detect uncaught exceptions, unnecessary catch and throws clauses effectively.

Static analysis techniques, however, cannot provide information about actual execution. So, dynamic analysis techniques have also been studied to provide information about actual execution [4, 13, 14]. Several dynamic analysis tools are developed for Java including J2ME Wireless Toolkit [14] and AdaptJ [13]. Recent J2ME Wireless Toolkit can trace method calls, exceptions and class loading as well as memory usage using JVMPI. However, it provides just the names of exceptions whenever exceptions are thrown. Moreover, JVMPI imposes heavy burden on performance overhead, which makes execution speed too slow. It is hard to trace interesting parts of programs effectively, because all codes including libraries are included in the trace. AdaptJ don't provide any exception-related information during execution.

Our current work differs from the previous static works in that the previous works focus on estimating uncaught exceptions rather than providing information on the propagation paths of thrown exceptions. Our monitoring system can trace in real-time how thrown exceptions including unchecked exceptions are handled and propagated during execution. This trace function has not been supported by any dynamic systems yet.

7   Conclusion

We have developed a dynamic exception monitoring system, which can help programmers trace and handle exceptions effectively. Using this system, programmers can examine exception handling process in more details by tracing only interesting exceptions, and can handle exceptions more effectively. To reduce performance overhead, we have designed the system based on inlined reference monitor. We are extending this system in two directions. The first one is to visualize exception trace and profile information, which can give more insights to programmers. The second one is to adapt this system to J2ME programs, which are widely used in mobile environment.

References

1. B. Bokowski, Andre Spiegel. Barat A Front-End for Java. Technical Report B-98-09 December 1998.
2. B.-M. Chang, J. Jo, K. Yi, and K. Choe, Interprocedural Exception Analysis for Java, *Proceedings of ACM Symposium on Applied Computing*, pp 620-625, Mar. 2001.
3. J.-D. Choi, D. Grove, M. Hind, and V. Sarkar, Efficient and precise modeling of exceptions for analysis of Java programs, *Proceedings of '99 ACM SIGPLAN-SIGSOFT Workshop on Program Analysis for Software Tools and Engineering*, September 1999, pp. 21-31.
4. B. Dufour, K. Driesen, L. Hendren and C. Verbrugge. Dynamic Metrics for Java. *Proceedings of ACM OOPSLA '03*, October, 2003, Anaheim, CA.
5. S. Drossopoulou, and T. Valkevych, Java type soundness revisited. Techical Report, Imperial College, November 1999. Also available from: http://www-doc.ic.ac.uk/ scd.
6. U. Erlingsson, *The inlined reference monitor approach to secure policy enforcement*, Ph.D thesis, Cornell University, January 2004.
7. E. Gamma, R. Helm, R. Johnson and J. Vlissides, *Design Patterns:Elements of Reusable Object-Oriented Software*, Addison-Wesley,1995.
8. J. Gosling, B. Joy, and G. Steele, *The Java Programming Language Specification*, Addison-Wesley,1996.
9. M. P. Robillard and G. C. Murphy, Analyzing exception flow in Java programs, in *Proc. of '99 European Software Engineering Conference and ACM SIGSOFT Symposium on Foundations of Software Engineering*, pp. 322-337.
10. B. G. Ryder, D. Smith, U. Kremer, M. Gordon, and N. Shah, A static study of Java exceptions using JESP, Tech. Rep. DCS-TR-403, Rutgers University, Nov. 1999.
11. S. Sinha and M. Harrold, Analysis and testing of programs with exception-handling constructs, *IEEE Transations on Software Engineering* 26(9) (2000).
12. K. Yi and B.-M. Chang Exception analysis for Java, ECOOP Workshop on Formal Techniques for Java Programs , June 1999, Lisbon, Portugal.
13. AdaptJ:A Dynamic Application Profiling Toolkit for Java, http://www.sable.mcgill.ca/ bdufou1/AdaptJ
14. Sun Microsystems, J2ME Wireless Toolkit, http://java.sun.com.

Distributed Exception Handling: Ideas, Lessons and Issues with Recent Exception Handling Systems

Aurélien Campéas[1], Christophe Dony[1], Christelle Urtado[2],
and Sylvain Vauttier[2]

[1] LIRMM, 161 rue ADA, 34392 Montpellier
[2] LGI2P, Ecole des Mines d'Alès, site EERIE,
Parc scientifique G. Besse, 30035 Nîmes

Abstract. Exception handling is an important feature of the tool-set that enables the building of fault-tolerant concurrent and distributed programs. While transactional distributed systems have been studied for a long time, distributed exception handling techniques are only now evolving towards maturity, especially within asynchronous multi agents or component based systems. In this paper, we review two recent proposals for distributed exceptions handling systems (DEHS), namely SaGE and Guardian, in the light of what the Erlang programming language brings to the table : native constructs for concurrency, distributedness and exception handling across processes. We expand on the merits and possible drawbacks of these systems. We advocate the need to introduce the notion of *resumption*, an often downplayed feature of EHSs, to modern day DEHS, in order to address the problem of multi agent systems facing the "real world".

1   Introduction

Exception handling mechanism have been a feature of programming languages for about thirty years now. The complete feature set of an exception handling system (EHS) is well known and stable (chap.1.1) in the context of non-concurrent, non-distributed programs [1, 2, 3, 4]. Yet within concurrent and distributed systems, it remains an active research topic [5].

Distributed computing has been addressed in length, with relation to programming languages. On one hand, distributed systems have been built with languages without any support for it except system call level primitives for process instantiation and message passing (like C or C++). On the other hand, actor's model programming language have been devised to make distribution and concurrency high-level and first-class concepts available to the programmer (recent examples : *Erlang* [6], *JoCaml* [7], *Oz* [8]). Thus, it is no surprise that in those recent languages we find building blocks, and even potent implementations of distributed EHS. We will begin to review the most mature of them, Erlang.

N. Guelfi (Ed.): RISE 2004, LNCS 3475, pp. 82–92, 2005.

There seems to be a middle ground between those poles, around Java. Java has already its own primitives to help building multi-threaded and distributed (RMI) programs. But in Java, there is no language support to manage exception handling across thread groups and process boundaries.

Thus, in this paper, we also review two proposals around this limitation of the Java platform : the *SaGE* [9, 10] and *Guardian* [11, 12, 13] systems, which specify and implement a DEHS for asynchronous component based and multi agents [14] systems written in Java. We believe that Erlang, SaGE and Guardian present important insights for the future makers of a DEHS. The CA Action framework is not reviewed there, for we lack sufficient knowledge about it, but it should nevertheless be mentioned.

As a programming language feature, an EHS is mostly orthogonal to other language features, but can be disastrous in the presence of low-level memory management primitives, like in C++, for instance. Similarly, it remains to be seen upon which assumptions it may behave well in distributed and concurrent settings. Through this study, we uncover some of them.

Finally, we advocate a DEHS supporting the notion of resumption of a computation after an exception has been handled.

1.1   The EHS Feature Set

Before we delve in DEHS, let us remember the commonly accepted features of an EHS [15]. Firstly, EHSs have been devised in the context of functional and imperative programming languages, which all carry the notion of a program execution as a sequential series of jumps from current continuation to next normal continuation.

An EHS introduces the notion of an exceptional set of continuations to be executed in the presence of an exceptional situation arising during a computation.

The act of *signaling* is what occurs when a program encounters an exceptional situation. It can be triggered automatically, by perusal of some built-in exception-throwing primitive, or explicitly via some signalment primitive. Signaling implies the building of an *exception object* carrying run-time information about the exceptional situation, and finding the innermost exception handler matching its type.

Exception handlers (EH) allow to define, at any arbitrary point in a program, a new set of exceptional continuations, that adds up to, or overrides part of, the current set ; each exceptional continuation is usually selected using the type of the exception object that is built at signalment time ; an EH has typically dynamic extent and global scope[1].

Most programming language since the past twenty five years, from Ada [16] to Java [17] or Haskell [18], have had this kind of exception handling capabilities, which is also referred to as the "termination" model. Indeed, the research of handlers is done "destructively", that is the call stack is unwound up to the handler to be selected.

---

[1] Some systems offer statically (class) or lexically scoped handlers.

The possibility to resume activity after signalment exists in the *"resumption"* model, where the signalment is merely a function call. The ability to resume depends on the type of the exception being signaled (an *error* implying termination, and a *continuable error*, or mere *condition*[2], allowing resumption). Thus, a handler may have the choice between termination (then the stack will be unwound up to the handler) or a list of possible resumption points, also described in the Common Lisp terminology as *restarts* [19]. Let us define the notion of restart.

Restarts are a set of continuations whose goal is to provide lexical reparation and resumption capabilities to an EHS. Restarts, being closed over one of the lexical environments located between the signaling place and the innermost last EH, can be told to modify their closed-over environment and do a non-local jump to this environment in order to resume the computation, if abortion is not wanted. They are typically selected and funcalled by an exception handler as the last step in the signalment cycle. Restarts have also dynamic extent and global scope.

Resumption is successfully supported in dynamic languages (mainly Smalltalk [4, 20] and various Lisps). To our knowledge, only Common Lisp and Dylan have restarts, which give a choice of resumption points. We will argue in the last chapter in favor of the resumption model in the context of distributed and concurrent programs.

1.2   Implications of This Feature Set

The main assumptions under which EHS have been built are:

- functional or imperative programming languages (where the notion of continuation makes sense),
- automatic memory management (garbage-collected languages),
- one single control flow,
- synchronous calls (or jumps) between parts of a program,
- determinism of execution and total-orderliness of any program's trace[3].

Distribution and concurrency raise new specific and difficult issues for fault-tolerance that have up to now remained incompletely studied.

1.3   Properties of Distributed, Concurrent Systems

Distributed and concurrent systems are build from small sequential and process-like blocks ; those blocks may be executed independently and concurrently, as long as they don't interact ; they may be distributed on different places, physically speaking ; they may have to cooperate in various ways to achieve a desired outcome : then, communication happens through asynchronous message passing.

---

[2] "A condition is a generalisation of an error" [19].

[3] This one has to be taken with a grain of salt. Haskell has a simple exception handling mechanism that works in spite of the lazy evaluation strategy ; however it needed a pinch of cleverness to get it working.

[21] identifies three concurrency patterns:

1. disjoint concurrency, where concurrent activities share nothing and do not synchronize (in the manner of independent UNIX processes),
2. competitive concurrency, where different running activities compete for some shared resources (like in the case of transactional systems),
3. cooperative concurrency, where different active entities act collectively to reach a common outcome.

Sometimes it seems like the distinction between the problem of one system's consistency and the handling of distributed, concurrent exceptions, is blurred. We defend the view that exception handling is a low-level construct which ought to remain orthogonal, albeit compatible, with transactional systems. Both are important with relation to software reliability and fault-tolerance, but they really are independent things. From now on, we will mainly focus on cooperative concurrency, without after-thoughts about transactions. Thus, we will not cover the Coordinated Atomic Action (CAA) framework [22, 23, 24] for it mixes those two aspects. We must note however that CA Actions embody most of the idea we will discuss here.

In the context of cooperative concurrency, the questions we face are:

- how to deal with asynchronous message-passing,
- how to design signalment path and boundaries, and exception handlers scope.

Older proposals, such as Guide or Argus [25], helped raise the importance of the notion of *concertation* amongst a set of cooperating entities. As we will show, SaGE and Guardian have retained this notion.

2   An Overview of Three Systems

Erlang is a high-level programming language with built-in features to provide fault-tolerance to massively concurrent and distributed programs. It is a complete, integrated system. It has been proven in the field [6].

On the other hand, SaGE and Guardian are independent of any language. But it must be noted that they fill an important gap in the Java world and their current implementations are purely Java based.

2.1   Erlang

Erlang has been built out of the need of an efficient, robust and massively parallel programming language for the programming of world-class telecoms switches; it has proven successful with relation to these objectives.

Language Constructs. At its core, Erlang is a pure *functional* programming language (i.e closures and function calls are everything) with a simple EHS providing exception signalment and handling but no resumption.

Erlang has a notion of *process*, which is an independent, distributable sequential piece of code. Erlang processes communicate through asynchronous message passing : no shared state is ever allowed between concurrent entities.

There are two types of processes : worker and supervisor processes. A typical Erlang program is a tree of supervisor processes whose leaf nodes are worker processes. At run time, the program is unfolded from the root supervisor process (which can be seen as the "main" process) to the leaves made of worker processes. The act of creating a new process, and message passing between processes, are always explicit.

Exception Handling. Whenever an exception is signaled (typically in a worker process), it can be handled within the process, with the classical set of operators ; if it isn't handled there, then the process automatically sends a message carrying failure notification to its direct supervisor - the last step in signalment - and suicides. Depending of the signaling process's expected durability (permanent, transient or temporary), it is restarted *from scratch* by its supervisor or nothing happens. Additionally, processes can be *linked* in a way that guarantees that whenever one process crashes, all associated processes also die. Thus, one unhandled exception can lead to a whole process group crash (and possibly a reboot by a supervisor).

Thus, a well-written Erlang program has its functionality distributed into a tree structured hoard of independent worker processes, such as to limit the consequences of a process crash (an unhandled exception) to a subtree, or a cluster of disjoint subtrees (by means of process linkage).

Conclusions. This has proven to be a very efficient, allegedly because simple, strategy for Erlang's initial target, namely the software running massive telecoms switches. Also while the Erlang EHS offer simple primitives, it allows the making of very complex systems by way of composition of those primitives.

2.2   SaGE

SaGE is a specialized DEHS, in that it first defines a protocol, in other words a fixed set of interactions between groups of concurrent and (possibly) distributed entities, and then defines a proper EHS on this protocol, which is named "service". SaGE has been implemented for the Madkit [26] multi agents system and the Jonas J2EE [27] component-based framework.

Services. A service is basically modelled after method invocation in object oriented languages ; it associates an agent, a name, a set of formal parameters and a piece of functionality. A service is said to be provided by an agent A, invoked by an agent B, and then executed by agent A.

There are however important differences with method invocation. In a non-concurrent object-oriented program, there is a call chain of method invocations; with services, there is a tree of services invocations.

This is because:

- one agent can execute in parallel many instances of any service (mapping to an even number of service invocations by possibly different agents),
- one service execution which invokes another service execution (it is then said to be a "complex" service) is not synchronously stuck to its normal or exceptional outcome, but can err on its own and indeed invocate many other sub-services, for the sake of redundancy or merely for it is profitable to exploit the distributedness of the agents, making the worst-case execution time the maximum of the execution of the distributed sub-services instead of the sum.

Such a protocol is said to be "semi-synchronous", that is an invoking process is free to do whatever it pleases until some later time when it decides to collect the answers, which it is, contractually, bound to do. This is much like Multilisp's "futures" [28].

Exception Handling. On a call-tree degenerated into a chain (or stack), the EHS behaves quite like in a monolithic Java program. There is a new type of exception : *SageException* ; for each service, one can associate a set of handlers with any set of subtypes of SageException.

In the general case, there is an important piece of functionality available that does not belong to the EHS of non concurrent systems. We have said that one service can issue many sub-service invocations for the sake of redundancy ; when doing this, one does not want to have our service execution killed because just one (or a few amongst many) redundant sub-service execution failed and signaled an exception ; instead it is practical to craft a special function that filters the exceptions and can decide not to handle or propagate upwards, that is to merely do nothing special and go on with the computation. This function is named the *"concertation"* function [29].

Limits and Conclusion. We can model a problem with SaGE as long as it fits well into the notion of service. That is, it works well for any problem for which a functional decomposition comes in handily like, for instance, information retrieval systems.

Indeed, SaGE tries hard to put the least possible amount of ordering constraints on the execution of services, in order to benefit as much as possible of concurrency of the executions. The only constraint is that a service execution starts before any of its sub-services, and terminates only after all of them have terminated. Thus, when service execution side-effects an agent's mental state or the outer world, then suddenly every kind of interlocking and race conditions raise its head ; at this point, the programmer has to cope with the ordering and serialisation of access to the shared entities through low level constructs like locks and mutexes, which are hard to get right and may have scalability issues. To avoid these issues, one must use a transactional system along with SaGE.

While restricted in various ways, SaGE is nevertheless an efficient and expressive framework that provides a simple DEHS on top of an oo-like interaction model.

2.3 Guardian

While SaGE defines a DEHS upon a set of well defined interactions, Guardian strives to be a complete DEHS, in the sense that it can work with any protocol for which an exception handling strategy can make sense. This mighty goal seems to be attained with Guardian, but at a price ; we will see how and why soon.

Components and Primitives. A multi-agent system extended with Guardian has two main new components : a special agent named "leader", and sets of agents engaged in a collective activity, whose members are said to be "participants". It adds to the participants a set of primitives to manage the exception handling whose scope is the collective activity. Exception handling at the level of a set of participants is said to be global ; accordingly, Guardian introduces a *GlobalException* sub hierarchy to the built-in exception taxonomy, like with SaGE and its SageException.

Those primitives mimic the Java EHS model, with one addition: methods to enable and disable local *contexts*. Contexts are a generalisation of the lexical context, from the viewpoint of exception handling of the monolithic EHSs; in those, it is easy to think about the places where signaling and handling happen: all EHSs provide syntax to help the programmer map an exception handler or a signaling instruction to their lexical contours. Guardian contexts represent phases of the program, those phases being now decoupled from the block structure of the programming language. Moreover, Guardian, being built on Java, cannot benefit from any syntactic sugar ; therefore it has to make context management available to the programmer through the "{enable|disable}Context" pair of primitives.

So, when writing an application exploiting the capabilities of Guardian, one has to think about the specification of the participants, which are bound to use the Guardian primitives to stack up contexts, to install exception handlers on those contexts and to signal global exceptions ; and about the leader, which computes the set of exceptions to be handled in the participants in response to a set of concurrent global exceptions.

According to the authors, the gist of exception handling is the choice of the "semantically correct" global exception to be signaled by a participant, so as to allow the leader to compute a meaningful concerted exception set in return. Off course, the choice depends heavily on the type or structure of the collective activity.

The Signalment Process. Signaling is a two phases mechanism, after a first global exception is signaled:

1. the leader is alerted, tells every other participant to suspend any work and wait synchronously for instructions, and then it collects all pending global exceptions,

2. when all the participants are ready, the leader computes a set of concerted exceptions to be raised in the participants in response to the set of global exception it has received, then it sends the computed exceptions back to the participants, which can then enter their handler and go on with their (concurrent) activities.

We should note that the leader is akin to the concertation function from SaGE: concertation is the central mechanism in Guardian whereas it is an auxiliary mechanism in SaGE.

Limits and Conclusion. Guardian has been built to address many, if not all, of the situations a DEHS has to cope with. For instance, services (like in SaGE), coordinated atomic actions (CAA) and conversations can be built using the Guardian framework.

But it does not scale well : the need to freeze all participants' activity whenever a global exception is signaled makes it not usable when the participant set becomes big or if some participants have to perform some uninterruptible, high-priority or real-time service. Moreover, the system would be sensible to crashes or unavailability of the leader ; uniqueness of the leader seems like a weak point.

Furthermore, one important problem remains the complexity of the system, for it is quite hard to figure out how to use it properly.

These two points relate to the fact that Guardian is more than a DEHS framework and seems to encourage the programmer to build transactional-like systems using exception handling capabilities, since those come with automatic agent synchronisation for free. In fact, there is probably a wrong coupling between EHS semantics and execution serialisation : both should probably not come in the same package, and under the same name.

3   The Case for Resumption

There is an emerging pattern around these systems : the global activity of the cooperative entities is well handled if it is spread in a tree of contexts ; exception handling in this case is, in part due to the notion of concertation, now well understood.

But the three systems lack the ability to resume an activity *around* the signaling point. While there are many reasons for not wanting to use an EHS with resumption, even in the context of non-concurrent, non-distributed programs[4], there are nevertheless good reasons to want it : we want to show there exists a world in which a DEHS with resumption is a good thing. First, we will see why Erlang hasn't got it, then why it is potentially usefull.

3.1   Erlang Philosophy: "Fail Fast"

The designers of Erlang provided an in-depth explanation for their design choices and why there is no resumption in Erlang : they had to built software that run

---

[4] See the main book on fault tolerance by Anderson & Lee.

continuously for years without interruption, and allowing incremental live upgrades. To get this, they devised a simple but expressive language (thus functional), with strong grips on massive concurrency and distributedness (hence the notion of processes as part of the language) and advanced serviceability and reliability features (thus, amongst many other features, a *simple, terminal* exception handling system).

The "fail fast" strategy embodied by Erlang has its roots in the early work on high-reliability systems (such as Tandems systems). Resumption may add complexity to the code and rarely tested code paths. In the context of hundred of thousands of concurrently running processes, it is wise to keep it simple, stupid, and be just brutal : when a process or a group of process is in fault, we had better "reboot" it, in the hope that it will work. And it just works.

But it works in the context of telecoms switches, which exposes the real world to the software in a (we believe) limited and controlled manner. The cost of rebooting a subtree of the running application may be, in those circumstances, lower than the maintenance burden of more complicated (and thus potentially bug-ridden) code paths.

We argue, with no more tools than common sense, that in some cases, resumption would be of great help.

3.2   Usefullness of Resumption

There are two sides to the arguments : some non-fatal conditions may have to be signaled, and some long-running processes had better not been restarted from scratch in the presence of non-fatal conditions.

Condition Handling. A terminating DEHS can only help dealing with hard, uncorrectable errors. In practice, there are a lot of non-error conditions that are to be dealt with, or possibly just ignored. The more a system is open to "real world" entities, the more it has to deal with those conditions. When some condition can be safely ignored by some program, we need a way to say "I don't care" in no more words.

Sometimes, these conditions have to be taken seriously : someone ought to plug in this network cable again, so that we can go on with our current work set. We need a way to be notified that something is going wrong, yet ask for a reparation by a different entity, and just resume work after reparation.

Resilience of Long-Running Processes. Very often, smallish conditions will grow, if unhandled, into proper errors. That is because they are causally linked : a non-erroneous low batteries notification shortly precedes a fatal power outage, if nothing is done in time. So we have to correct the small glitches in order to prevent the bigger breakages. This is even more needed in distributed and concurrent systems facing the real world, that is, a lot of unexpected albeit not yet deadly events.

To sum up, whenever a robot, in a factory, experiences an exceptional and locally unsolvable situation, we don't think that destroying the robot and replacing it is a good way to handle the problem.

4   Conclusion

Resumption is a useful feature that prevent, where needed, a lot of ad-hockery. We may need it in the future DEHS. It would be an interesting experiment to bring them to Erlang, or to extend Common Lisp with primitives to deal, *à la* Erlang, with issues of concurrency and distributedness.

References

1. Weinreb, D.L.: Signalling and handling conditions. Technical report, Symbolics, Inc., Cambridge, MA (1983)
2. Koenig, A.R., Stroustrup, B.: Exception handling for C++. In: Proceedings "C++ at Work" Conference. (1989)
3. Pitman, K.: Exceptional situations in lisp. In: EUROPAL'90. (1990)
4. Dony, C.: A fully object-oriented exception handling system : Rationale and smalltalk implementation. In Romanovsky, A., Dony, C., Knudsen, J.L., Tripathi, A., eds.: Advances in Exception Handling Techniques. LNCS (Lecture Notes in Computer Science) 2022, Springer-Verlag (2001)
5. Romanovsky, A., Dony, C., Knudsen, J.L., A.Tripathi: Advances in Exception Handling Techniques. LNCS (Lecture Notes in Computer Science) 2022. Springer-Verlag (2001)
6. Armstrong, J.: Making Reliable Distributed Systems in the presence of Software Errors. PhD thesis (2003)
7. Sylvain Conchon, F.L.F.: Jocaml : mobile agents for objective caml. (1999)
8. Peter Van Roy, S.H.: Mozart, a programming system for agents applications. (1999)
9. Souchon, F., Dony, C., Urtado, C., Vauttier, S.: A proposition for exception handling in multi-agent systems. In: SELMAS'03 International Worskshop proceedings. (2003)
10. Frédéric Souchon, Sylvain Vauttier, C.U.C.D.: Fiabilité des applications multi-agents : le système de gestion d'exception sage. (2004)
11. Tripathi, A., Miller, R.: Exception handling in agent-oriented systems. In Romanovsky, A., Dony, C., Knudsen, J.L., Tripathi, A., eds.: Advances in Exception Handling Techniques. LNCS (Lecture Notes in Computer Science) 2022, Springer-Verlag (2001)
12. Miller, R., Tripathi, A.: Primitives and mechanisms of the guardian model for exception handling in distributed systems. In: Exception Handling in Object Oriented Systems: towards Emerging Application Areas and New Programming Paradigms Workshop (at ECOOP'03 international conference) proceedings. (2003)
13. Miller, R.: The Guardian Model for Exception Handling in Distributed Systems. PhD thesis (2003)
14. Ferber, J.: Multi-Agent Systems: An Introduction to Distributed Artificial Intelligence. (Addison-Wesley Pub Co; 1st edition (February 25, 1999))
15. Goodenough, J.B.: Exception handling: Issues and a proposed notation. Communications of the ACM **18** (1975) 683–696
16. J. Ichbiah, J.G.P. Barnes, J.H.B.K.B.O.R.B.W.: Rationale for the design of the ada programming language. In: ACM Sigplan Notices. Volume 14(6B). (1979)
17. Sun Microsystems Mountain View, Calif.: Java 2 Platform, Standard Edition (J2SE). (2004) http://java.sun.com/j2se.

18. Jones, S.P.: Tackling the awkward squad : monadic input/output, concurrency, exceptions and foreign-language calls in haskell. (2002)
19. Pitman, K.: Condition handling in the lisp language family. In: Advances in Exception Handling Techniques. (2001)
20. Dony, C.: Exception handling and object-oriented programming : towards a synthesis. ACM SIGPLAN Notices **25** (1990) 322–330 *OOPSLA/ECOOP '90 Proceedings*, N. Meyrowitz (editor).
21. Romanovsky, A.B., Kienzle, J.: Action-oriented exception handling in cooperative and competitive concurrent object-oriented systems. In: Advances in Exception Handling Techniques. (2001) 147–164
22. Romanovsky, A.B.: Conversations of objects. Computer Languages **21** (1995) 147–163
23. Wu, B.R.A.R.C.R.C.R.S.Z., Xu, J.: From recovery blocks to concurrent atomic actions. In: Predictably Dependable Computing Systems. ESPRIT Basic Research Series (1995) 87–101
24. Romanovksy, A., Kienzle, J.: Action-oriented exception handling in cooperative and competitive object-oriented systems. In Romanovsky, A., Dony, C., Knudsen, J.L., Tripathi, A., eds.: Advances in Exception Handling Techniques. LNCS (Lecture Notes in Computer Science) 2022, Springer-Verlag (2001) Also available as Technical Report (EPFL-DI No 00/346).
25. Liskov, B.: Distributed programming in argus. In: Communications of the ACM, vol. 31, n°3. (1988) 300–312
26. Jacques Ferber, O.G.: Madkit: Organizing heterogeneity with groups in a platform for multiple multi-agent systems. (1997)
27. : Java open application server (JOnAS) 4.1 : a J2EE platform (2004) http://www.objectweb.org/jonas/current/doc/JOnASWP.html.
28. Halstead, R., Loaiza, J.: Exception handling in multilisp. In: 1985 Int'l. Conf. on Parallel Processing. (1985) 822–830
29. Issarny, V.: Concurrent exception handling. In: Advances in Exception Handling Techniques. (2001)

A Model Based Approach to Design Applications for Network Processor

S. Afsharian[3,4], A. Bertolino[1], G.De Angelis[1], P. Iovanna[3], and R. Mirandola[2]

[1] Istituto di Scienza e Tecnologie,
dell'Informazione "Alessandro Faedo" CNR,
Via G. Moruzzi 1, I–56124 Pisa, Italy
{antonia.bertolino, guglielmo.deangelis}@isti.cnr.it
[2] Dip. di Informatica,Sistemi e Produzione,
Università di Roma "Tor Vergata" 00113 Roma, Italy
raffaela@info.uniroma2.it
[3] Ericsson Lab Italy,
Via Anagnina 203, 00040 Roma - Italy
{sharareh.afsharian, paola.iovanna}@ericsson.com
[4] Dipartimento di Informatica,
Università di L'Aquila,
Via Vetoio, Coppito, L'Aquila ,67010 (Italy)

Abstract. Network Processors (NPs) are an emerging class of embedded systems used in the telecommunication domain for applications like routing and switching. In this paper we introduce the main characteristics of the existing NP architectures and the difficulties intrinsic to their software application design. On the other hand we review the basic principles underlying the well-known model-based development (MBD) approach. After motivating the opportunity of applying MBD to the domain of NPs, we outline a framework currently under development for the application of MBD to the design of NP software applications, thus allowing for the early derivation of test plans and for performance analysis.

1 Introduction

With the growing relevance and pervasiveness of telecommunications, a good deal of interest has been recently drawn by the study of Network Processors (NPs) since they play an important role in the design of modern routers. In simple terms, NPs are specialized embedded systems looking for a middle ground between totally hard-coded solutions on one side and general purpose programmable devices on the opposite one. Designing software applications for NP architectures can not be an easy task since such processors are required to process packets at high line speeds, support complex packet processing functions, and at the same time be programmable so to incorporate new functionality. To support such stringent demands, most network processors available today consist of a collection of heterogeneous processing elements, memory subsystems and on-chip communication infrastructure.

N. Guelfi (Ed.): RISE 2004, LNCS 3475, pp. 93–101, 2005.

Dealing with the diversity of technological solutions, the heterogeneity of processing elements and the possibly distributed software design in the application design phase is very hard. There are mainly two possible approaches to design an application for NPs:

1. To rely on some well-known provider without worrying about heterogeneity
2. To accept the diversity of technological solutions as a fact and finding generic solution that take into account this heterogeneity problem.

The latter approach leads to the adoption of a new paradigm for system development, in which models and meta-models play a central role [17]. This line is now championed by several organizations [16] and is called Model-based Development (MBD).

The basic idea of MBD is to create a set of models that help the designers understand and evaluate both the system requirements and implementation. A model is a reduced abstract representation of the system that highlights some properties of interest in the considered phase and that is separate from specific properties of the execution environment. In such a way, the invariants of a business domain may be held apart from the implementation, preserving them from technology evolution. The models can be refined/extended in several ways to take into account the aspects of interest for the designers.

On the other hand these models share common concerns hence it is necessary to have some tool allowing bridging them together. Meta-modeling technology is suggested as a good solution to allow addressing this issue in a very efficient way.

In this context, we have launched a research initiative to investigate the applicability of models and meta-models in the context of embedded systems and in particular on NPs. Specifically, we outline here a new approach for the design of NP software applications based on the definition of different models, at different abstraction levels, for the NP application and the underlying architecture. The whole NP model is then defined by the combinations of the derived/separated models.

In the next two sections we provide some background information about the technologies we use, namely NP and MBD; in Section 4, we lay out an outline of the approach we are building towards model based development of NP; finally, we draw conclusions in Section 5.

2   NP Overview

Network devices are a growing class of embedded system and include traditional Internet equipment like routers, switches, and firewalls; newer devices like Voice over IP (VoIP) bridges, virtual private network (VPN) gateways, and quality of service (QOS) enforcers; and web-specific devices like caching engines, load balancers, and SSL accelerators.

Apart from different functionality, the major semiconductors board can be categorized as follow :

– ASIC : Application Specific Integrated Circuit, any hardwired solution
– ASIP: Application Specific Instruction Solution, an instruction set processor for a particular application domain
– Co-processor: An hardwired possibly configurable solution with limited programming interface

- FPGA: Field Programmable Gate Array, a device that can be reprogrammed at the gate level
- GPP: General Purpose Processor, a programmable processor for general purpose computing

Analyzing the flexibility and performance features of these classes, we can identify ASICs as the one that provides the highest performance but at the cost of the lowest flexibility; on the opposite side, GPPs result the most flexible class, but with the lowest performance. In the networking domain, ASIPs provide a good trade-off between hardware and software solutions, allowing the products to achieve a good balance between performance and flexibility.

An NP is a programmable device with architectural features for packet processing at rates of 1 Gbit/s and above; it is a particular ASIP in the previous classification [14]. The main network processor functions are: header classification; deep packet analysis; packet processing; policing and statistics; and traffic management.

In a field where high speed and performance rules, can seem strange to prefer a slower solution to an higher one. The main reasons for using a NP instead of ASIC can be found analyzing and comparing time to market (TTM) and time in market (TIM) for both technologies. TTM for an ASIC is quite long, and is not uncommon that its development time can holds over more than a year. Furthermore the net revolution, also to improve the band demand, yields to the creation of new services and to a more convergence among data and voice. ASIC hardwired nature does not allow to follow big changes, so its TIM can be relatively short. On the other hand, an NP chose some software solution over some hardware ones. It pays in performance in comparison with the ASIC but gains a shorter TTM and stretching the TIM allowing to upgrade software components.

Although a wide variety of NP architectures exists, they share some common features. A key point with all architectures is that they all employ multiple programmable processing engines (PPE) [2]. The main function of the NP is to process packet data at wire-speed, so the existence of PPEs. On the other hand an NP needs to manipulate control and management packets that generally don't need to be processed at such a high rate but have complex processing requirements. This reason leads to have a Control Processor Element (CPE) [2] which in some cases can execute simple control plane applications and is responsible of other functions such as booting or hosting interface. Besides, NPs, as any programmable devices, clearly also require memories to store programs, lookup table, packet or queue information. NPs supply a very compact internal memory that is mainly used to store the code for packet processing by the PPEs. However external memories are required to run applications; for these reasons NPs provide one or more external memory interfaces managed by controllers, often specialized for a particular role as queueing or table look-up handling. Data plane tasks require a small amount of code, but a large amount of processing power. In contrast, control plane tasks require little processing power, but a large amount of code. Many NPs provide also an interface to Fabric Switch (FS).

As well as the different solutions have some common hardware feature, recurrent languages approaches are used for programming network processors. Mainly, the C language or a variant of it is used to program the CPE and in some cases also the PPEs, although often for the latter an assembly approach is still preferred (like Intel or Motorola solutions) [11] [9]. Many PPEs, in fact, have an architecture that is not a good target for a C program, lacking for example a support for pointers in its instructions set. Moreover the code is too hardware dependent, including register swapping or clock cycles waiting. Finally, there are some families of NPs that allow to program their elements by means of functional or 4th generation programming languages (like Agere solution) [1]. The reason of this choice is because classification is an important part of NP software, and this kind of operations can be simply described by means of rules applicable under specified conditions.

3   Model Based Development

Model based development is a new approach to software development in which the focus and the primary artifacts of development are models (instead of programs). A model can be seen as "a reduced representation of some system that highlights the properties of interest from a given viewpoint" [4][5]. In such a way we don't see everything at once and we use a representation that can be easily understood for the objective of the study at the given stage. The importance of models is a well recognized fact in several fields of engineering (e.g., mechanical, civil, or naval engineering) and also in some areas of computer science such as performance and reliability engineering [10] [13] [8]. Models are fundamentals to help the understanding of complex systems and are useful for all the phases of the system life cycle: from requirements to design to implementation. The use of models minimizes risk by detecting errors and omissions early in the design cycle, and improves the overall quality of the obtained system. Indeed models can be evaluated through analysis and experimentation and are useful to investigate and compare alternative solutions, to communicate understanding to different stakeholders and to drive implementation. A useful model should be abstract (with respect to the modeled system) but on the same time it should faithfully represent the modeled system. It should be easily understandable, simply solvable to answer questions about the modeled system and obtainable with very low cost with respect to the system [10] [5] [13].

MBD is a top-down process as illustrated in Fig.1.

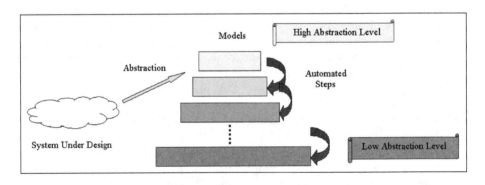

Fig. 1. MDB Top Down Approach

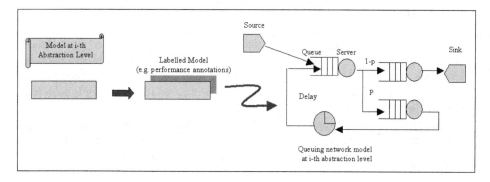

Fig. 2. MBD: an horizontal refinement

The underlying philosophy is to begin by identifying the principal elements of the system and the ways in which they interact, and then supply any details that prove to be necessary. In other words this means that a large number of assumptions will be introduced and assessed in the process of conducting a modeling study. There is a strong incentive to identify and eliminate details that will not have a primary impact on the results of the study. The obtained model is then refined continuously until the desired level of details is obtained. The refinement steps, in some application field, could be automated and different models should conform to the overall meta-model. Note that several high-level models can be obtained as a starting point of this top-down approach according to the objective of the study. A widely used approach, for example, is to distinguish from the first steps the application and the architecture of the system so generating separate high-level models [12] [6].

The integration of different models at possibly different levels of abstraction is the key point to obtain high quality and efficient system design. Integration is concerned on a vertical level (Fig.1) as well as on a horizontal level (Fig.2). In this latter case, starting from a model at a given abstraction level it is possible to provide some refinements guided by the objective of the study. We can study, for example, the performance of the system building performance models and solving them using some automated methodology proposed for this goal [20] [6]. A horizontal approach can be useful also to apply an aspect-oriented development approach [15], where different aspects can be seen as different refinement of an original model.

Fig. 2 illustrates a horizontal refinement versus performance models: the original model is augmented with performance annotations and then after a series of transformation a performance model is obtained (a queuing network [10] in this example). Similar refinements can be done for the analysis of other system quality attributes.

Another important aspect in the MBD is the assessment of the *goodness* of a model, i.e., how close the model is to the real system. This involves a verification step ensuring that the model is correctly built and a validation step ensuring that the model produces results close to those observed in the real system.

4   MBD Applied to NPs

As already stated designing an application for an NP can be a very hard work: design-ers have to identify both software algorithms and their distribution on NP hardware resources. As the NPs consist of different processors and also contain dedicated co-processors a true concurrent programming style is required for managing synchroniza-tion and performance aspects.

Following the ideas proposed in [12], we intend to explore the possibility to apply a MBD approach to the design of NP applications, in particular we devise the Y-chart approach as the more suitable for such embedded software design.

The Y-chart [7] represents a general scheme for the design of heterogeneous systems. In the Y-chart a clear distinction is made between applications and architectures, which are related via an explicit mapping step. This concept is so general that it can be applied at various levels of abstraction and different kind of scenarios [3] [19].

The general scheme we propose to adopt for the design of an NP application is depicted in Fig. 3. Basically, when designing an application for NP, the first step is to decide which software architecture is best suited for the goal. The next step is to formalize the hardware architecture of the chosen NP and try to map each software component[1] on a specific element.

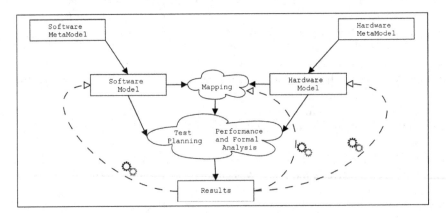

Fig. 3. Y-model schema for NP applications

Generally different NPs are built up by means of different hardware architecture. These differences can be explained in terms of technology, external interfaces, processing elements and connections among them. However we note that some recurrent high level concepts are common in a lot of real-world NP architectures. For this reason we would like to define a formal representation of the main characteristics of the NPs by means of a meta-model. This meta-model should consider some critical information about NP elements such as memory space, processor frequency or interfaces delay.

---

[1] In this paper we refer as *component* a software unit specialized for a role.

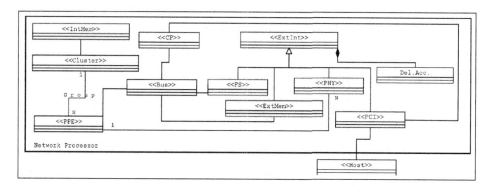

Fig. 4. A possible hardware meta-model

Fig.4 depicts a schema of a possible meta-model definition for the hardware side of the Y-model. As described in Sec. 2 a NP is generally build up by a *CPE* and some *PPE* that can be organized in *Clusters*. Each cluster can refer to a small internal memory (*IntMem*) and each PPE can send or receive data from the physical lines by means *PHY* interfaces. The CPE and the PPEs can interact with external devices (*ExtInt*) such as *FS*s or external memories (*ExtMem*) by means *Bus*es. Each external interfaces is characterized by a delay access time (*DelAcc*). An external *Host* is connected to the NP's CPE by means a *PCI* interface.

Since NPs are programmable but on the same time they are a very specialized hardware, therefore we believe that applications could have a common structure. Also on the software side, we would like to define a meta-model which can describe the high level concepts that are required by a NP software application. Software meta-model should describe for some elements useful information such as the estimated line of code for a component.

Both the previous high level definitions have to be intended as general and no focused on any particular solution, neither hardware or software. Our intent is to describe such meta-models by means of OMG's MOF [18].

Focusing on a particular NP, the first step is to create a model for the chosen platform that is consistent with the hardware meta-model. As a mirror image, on the other side of Y-model, a model for the particular software application must be created in conformity to its meta-model.

The core of our proposal is represented by the association between the software model and the hardware one. We believe that this mapping can be led by means of non-functional annotations like memory size or expected number of code lines for a component, that are stored into software and hardware models. When each software component is then bounded with an hardware element, we believe that performance estimation, test planning or some kind of application dependent formal analysis are possible during the design. According to this first analysis, the designers can decide to accept the solution or correct it acting toward a more correct mapping or a better model of the system.

The hardware and software models represent a static description of the whole system, but it is clear that for a complete application design also dynamic aspects are required.

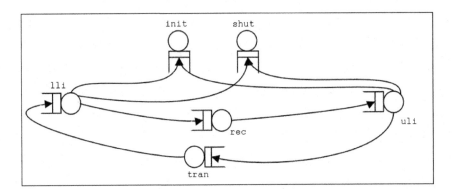

Fig. 5. A queuing network example

The software model should describe both the dynamic of a single software component and the data-flow among the different components.

To describe dynamic behaviors into a single software component, it is possible to use UML-based diagrams such as activity or sequence diagrams. These diagrams can then be augmented with performance annotations by expoliting a MBD horizontal development of the system.

To describe dynamic behaviors among different software components, we suppose that each component is distributed, so it runs on its own PPE. Under such hypothesis, a component can not exploit a classic simple function invocation to perform an action realized by a function that is implemented on another component. It is necessary to explicitly consider the data exchange. On the other hand, each software component can serve concurrently one or more other components, so it is necessary a container that provide a "waiting-room" service. For these reasons the idea we intend to investigate in this context is the possibility to use the queuing network modeling approach [10] to formalize the aspects related to the management of exchange of information in concurrent environment. In this case, we prefer queuing networks instead of classical UML, because the first provide explicit concepts to model such scenarios.

As an example let us consider an application that manages a connection oriented protocol, such as TCP or SCTP. The application can be structured as follow: a lower level (*lli*) and an upper level interface (*uli*) module, an initialization module (*init*) which helps to build up a new connection, a transmitter (*tran*) and a receiver (*rec*) module which respectively serves to elaborate data for sending and receiving, and finally a module that provides to shut down an existing connection (*shut*). Fig.5 shows a possible queuing network for this simple system. Guessing on the kind of the traffic such as the percentage of initialization or shutdown requests, transmitted and received packets, we would like to determinate and study the queue sizes and some first estimation about delay times.

We believe that the strength of our proposal is to give an high level and formal methodology that can allow a better application engineering in embedded systems like NPs. Modelling the applications in this manner according to the MBD approach, should make easier the test plan definition and allow to have at design time a first performance and formal analysis.

5   Conclusions and Future Works

This paper presents an on-going work whose goal is the definition of a model-based development approach for the design of software applications for network processors. Each of the two domains we are trying to combine, MBD and NPs, opens a new promising research fields in software system engineering. However, as they are both quite young domains, the investigation is still open in any direction, and their combination then poses even more difficult challenges and uncertainty. We have outlined here the seminal stage of an original approach that relies on, and adapts to a NP framework, the concepts and steps of the MBD technology. Future work includes of course a more detailed definition of the methodology and its application to case studies coming from the industrial world.

References

1. Agere. *The Challenge for Next Generation Network Processors*. White Paper.
2. A.Heppel. An introduction to network processors, January 2003.
3. B.Kienhuis, E.Deprettere, K.Vissers, and P.Van Der Wolf. An approach for quantitative analysis of application-specific dataflow architectures, August 04 1997.
4. B.Selic. The pragmatic of model-driven development. *IEEE Software*.
5. B.Selic. Model-driven development, uml 2.0, and performance engineering. In *Proceedings of the Fourth Int. Workshop on Software and Performance*. ACM, 2004. Invited talk WOSP2004.
6. C.U.Smith and L.Williams. *Performance Solutions: A practical Guide To Creating Responsive, Scalable Software*. Addison-Wesley, 2001.
7. D.Gajski and R.Kuhn. Guest Editors' introduction: New VLSI tools. *Computer*, 16(12):11–14, December 1983.
8. D.Hamlet, D.Mason, and D.Woit. Properties of software systems synthesized from components, June 2003. To appear as a book chapter. http://www.cs.pdx.edu/~hamlet/lau.pdf.
9. D.Husak. *Network Processors: A Definition and Comparison*. C-Port. White Paper.
10. E.D.Lazowska, J.Zahorjan, G.S.Graham, and K.C.Sevcik. *Quantitative System Performance. Computer Systems Analysis Using Queueing Network Models*. Prentice Hall, Inc., 1984.
11. Intel. *Intel IXP2400 Network Processor: Flexible, High-Performance Solution for Access and Edge Applications*. White Paper.
12. P.Boulet, J.Dekeyser, C.Dumoulin, and P.Marquet. Mda for soc design, intensive signal processing experiment. *FDL'03, Frankfurt am Main.ECSI*.
13. S.A.Hissam, G.A.Moreno, J.A.Stafford, and K.C.Wallnau. Packaging predictable assembly. *Lecture Notes in Computer Science*, 2370:108–124, 2002.
14. Niraj Shah. Understanding network processors. Master's thesis, University of California, Berkeley, September 2001.
15. The Aspect Oriented Software Development Web Site. http://aosd.net.
16. The MDA Web Site. http://www.omg.org/mda/.
17. The Model-Driven Software Development Web Site. http://www.mdsd.info.
18. The MOF Web Site. http://www.omg.org/mof/.
19. T.Stefanov, P.Lieverse, E.Deprettere, and P.Van Der Wolf. Y-chart based system level performance analysis: An M-JPEG case study, October 16 2000.
20. V.Cortellessa and R.Mirandola. Prima-uml: A performance validation incremental methodology on early uml diagrams. *Science of Computer Programming*, 44(1):101–129, jul 2002.

A MOF-Based Metamodel for SA/RT

Joakim Isaksson, Johan Lilius, and Dragos Truscan*

Embedded Systems Laboratory, Turku Centre for Computer Science,
Lemminkäisenkatu 14A, 20520 Turku, Finland

Abstract. We present a MOF-based metamodel for the SA/RT (Structured Analysis for Real-Time Systems) design method. The metamodel provides a well-defined interpretation of the SA/RT elements, allowing the designer to create unambiguous specifications of systems. The metamodel was designed to be easily combined with UML and UML tools, in order to provide support for creating, editing and manipulating SA/RT models in UML environments. The approach allowed us, to specify and implement automated model transformations both between SA/RT models and between SA/RT and UML models.

1   Introduction

In light of increasing complexity of today's embedded systems, model-driven development has become one of the necessary solutions to handle high complexity and to ensure consistency of the specifications at different steps during the development process. Usage of models allows designers to raise the level of abstraction and to use various views to describe the system at different levels of detail, thus shifting the focus from implementation concerns to solution modeling. To fully take advantage of a model-based approach, appropriate tool support is required. Not only means to (graphically) create, edit and manipulate model elements, but also scripting facilities to support automated manipulation and consistency checking of such models are required, in order to speed up the design process and to cut down development times.

Recently, OMG started to promote the Model-Driven Architecture (MDA) initiative [1]. The main idea behind MDA is to define and use well-defined models to represent the system, and model transformations to go from requirements to specific implementations, assisted by appropriate tools. The main modeling language of MDA is, unsurprisingly, represented by the Unified Modeling Language (UML) [2], but other languages can be addressed too. MDA suggests the Meta-Object Facility (MOF) [3] as the main language for defining modeling languages. A MOF model can be seen as a meta-model for other meta-models, or, using the standard metamodeling terminology, a meta-meta-model. The strength of a MOF-based metamodel resides in the possibility to define and integrate other graphical notations into UML tools, thus allowing creating, editing and manipulating of models in a graphical fashion.

One such modeling language is represented by the Structured Analysis for Real-Time Systems (SA/RT), a graphical design notation focused on analyzing the functional

---

* Support for this work from the HPY and TES research foundations is gratefully acknowledged.

N. Guelfi (Ed.): RISE 2004, LNCS 3475, pp. 102–111, 2005.

behavior and information flow through a system. Although one of the most frequently used methods in designing embedded applications, in recent years Structured Analysis has been largely overshadowed by UML and object-oriented methods. In our opinion, the supremacy of UML is largely due to the tool support it provides. However, we believe that structural methods provide, in certain situations, important advantages compared to object-oriented methods and that sometimes a combination of both is not only useful, but also fundamental for developing complex embedded systems [4]. We presented in [5] such a model-driven approach along with a discussion of the related work in combining object oriented and data flow views of the systems.

In this paper, we present a MOF-based metamodel for SA/RT that, by providing a well-defined interpretation of the SA/RT elements, enables the designer to create unambiguous representations of systems in a tool supported manner. The goal of this work was three fold: (1) to explore the flexibility of MOF in creating and using meta-languages; (2) to specify and implement a MOF metamodel for SA/RT that can be used either as a stand-alone tool or in combination with other MOF metamodels (e.g., UML) in a common modelling environment; (3) to investigate the support for implementing automated model transformations not only between models of the same metamodel, but also between models of distinct metamodels.

Following, the paper presents in Sect. 2 how the metamodel was defined and built starting from the SA/RT specification. Section 3 explains the metamodel implementation in our SMW tool along with the implementation decisions taken during the process. Short examples of scripts are given in Sect. 4 to illustrate how the MOF-based approach could be used to provide automation for model interrogation and manipulation, and to implement model transformations between different models. The paper ends with some concluding remarks.

2   A Metamodel for SA/RT

This section presents the SA/RT metamodel and the methodology used to develop it. One of our goals was to be able to incorporate data flow models and data flow information with UML models. We tried to keep the SA/RT metamodel as compatible with the UML metamodel as possible, although it also functions perfectly well as a stand-alone model. In practice, this means that the core framework of the metamodel is quite similar to the UML metamodel core, but with some unnecessary features removed, making the SA/RT metamodel directly connectable to the standard UML 1.4 metamodel.

2.1   The SA/RT Notation

One apparent problem when creating models using the SA/RT approach is that different tools and practitioners interpret the SA/RT notation in different ways [6], a fact which can give rise to inconsistencies and confusion. A well-defined metamodel for SA/RT could help to resolve such problems.

Since its introduction, several alternative interpretations of the SA/RT notation have been presented in the literature. To create a metamodel it is thus necessary to decide upon one interpretation of the standard. Our approach is to use the original specification by

Ward and Mellor [7] as the starting point and use it as far as possible. A second variant of the SA/RT notation was proposed by Hatley and Pirbhai [8], with the difference that it separates the dataflow and control information into two separate views, making in our opinion the models more difficult to understand. This is certainly not the only example of differences between the Hatley/Pirbhai and Ward/Mellor methodologies, for there are some minor notational differences in the definitions of the data-flow diagrams, but we think that the better clarity of the Ward/Mellor approach motivates our choice. The basic building blocks of a SA/RT system do remain the same regardless of the different notational dialects: systems are described using `data-flow diagrams`, `finite state machines` and `data dictionaries`. These are briefly described below.

Data Flow Diagram (DFD) is the main diagram used for structured analysis, modeling the data flow through the entire system along with the manipulations done to this data. A DFD consists of three main kinds of components: `transformations`, `stores`, and `flows`. A `transformation` performs some operation on the information it receives as input, after which the modified information is produced as output, while a `store` only stores the information it receives as input, eventually passing it on unmodified to another model element. `Flows` act as the glue of the system, connecting `transformations` and `stores` together and transporting the information between them. DFDs can (and should) be hierarchical, where the upmost layer is actually a context diagram describing the interfaces between the system and the outside world, and the `external entities` interacting with these interfaces. Lower layers then refine the system until the functionality of all transformations has been described.

An important and distinguishing characteristic of the DFD is the separation of data and control information, meaning that there are both control and data variants of the three main components listed above. `Control transformations` process control events, while `data transformations` process data or special control events (e.g., enabling and disabling the data transformations). Similarly, `data stores` and `data flows` only handle data, while their `control flows` counterparts only accept events. How to describe the functionality of the data transformations is not specified in detail in the literature, but typically this can be done using pseudocode or flowcharts. The functionality of `control transformations` is described using state machines. There are other rules regarding how different system components may be connected to each other, but due to space reasons we omit them here.

State Machines are used to model `control transformations`. The specification in [7] describes a rather simple state machine model, without any of the syntactic sugar found the statechart definition of UML (e.g., hierarchical and history states).

Data Dictionaries describe the data flowing through the system, where the contents and structure of each data element is described in detail. Ward and Mellor suggest a regular-expression like notation to denote this information, as the data may be refined into several smaller subsets of the original data type.

2.2   The Metamodel

The four main components in a MOF-based metamodel are: `packages`, `classes`, `associations` and `data types`. Meta-objects in the target metamodel are modeled using `classes`, while the `associations` model binary relationships between

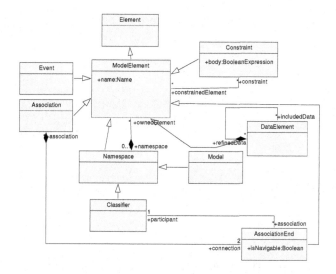

Fig. 1. The Core package of the SA/RT metamodel

these meta-objects. Data types model data such as primitive and external types. Packages are used to make the model more manageable by modularizing it. "Standard" object-oriented features are supported, i.e. classes may have attributes, inheritance and aggregation associations are included, etc. In practice, a MOF-based metamodel can be constructed in much the same way as one would construct any class diagram for an object-oriented design. Additional constraints on the metamodel can be specified through well-formedness rules which must hold in order for the model to be considered correct. The well-formedness rules which are defined for the MOF standard are expressed using the Object Constraint Language (OCL).

Our SA/RT metamodel is divided into six packages. The Core package contains fundamental metamodel elements needed by the other packages, while the Dataflow, ActivityGraph and StateMachine packages describe the actual diagrams of an SA/RT model. Additionally, we use the Auxiliary and Expressions packages to reduce the size of the Core package.

Since we wanted to retain the possibility to incorporate data flow modeling capabilities with UML, the Core package (Fig. 1) is essentially a subset of the UML core model. The main differences are the addition of the DataElement class, which represents the different types of data flowing through the system and which may in turn be subsets of other data types, and the simplification or omission of some constructs such as the Event class, which does not need the associated signature it has in the corresponding UML metamodel, as events do not carry any data values in SA/RT.

The Dataflow package (Fig. 2) defines the elements that may be included in a DFD. There are essentially three main classes and their subclasses that provide all the model elements allowed.

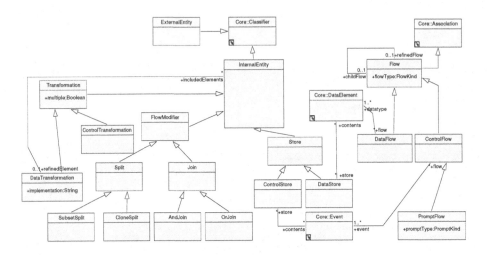

Fig. 2. The Dataflow package of the SA/RT metamodel

- The ExternalEntity class represents entities outside the system boundaries. Interacting through the system-level interfaces, these entities can provide input to the system or receive output from the system.
- The Flow class defines the flows between the transformations and stores in the DFD. The subclasses DataFlow and ControlFlow define flows for transporting data and events, respectively. The PromptFlow class models the special control flows enabling and disabling data transformations. The flowKind attribute specifies whether the flow is continuous or discrete, while the refinedFlow-childFlow association represents the connection between a flow in a higher-level DFD and the corresponding refined flow in the lower-level DFD.
- The InternalEntity class is used to define the Transformation, Store and FlowModifier elements, from which the elements of the DFDs are defined.

    - The subclasses of Transformation define DataTransformations and ControlTransformations. Their internal representation is specified by the StateMachine and ActivityGraph packages, respectively.
    - FlowModifier subclasses are used to model the connection points where the contents of a flow can be modified. Split either splits a flow into a number of identical copies (CloneSplit) or into a number of subsets (SubsetSplit) of the original flow. Join either joins the contents of several flows into one flow (AndJoin) or creates one flow containing one of the original flows (OrJoin).
    - ControlStore and DataStore model event and data repositories.

The Ward/Mellor book defines a very simplistic state machine structure for modeling control transformations, but there is of course nothing that prevents us from using some other, more complex, state machine model. Because of this, and because of our metamodel's compatibility with the UML core metamodel, we instead chose to use the statechart metamodel of UML as the basis for our StateMachine package, which defines the state machine part of the metamodel. Similarly, since the SA/RT specification does not impose a certain approach and because we wanted to employ a graphical approach, we decided to use, beside plain text, activity diagrams to represent the internals of the data transformations. We defined them in the `ActivityGraph` package. As these metamodels are essentially identical to the UML `stateChart` and UML `activityGraph` metamodels, we omit them here. We also omit the presentation of the `Auxiliary` and `Expressions` packages, but they can be found in [9].

In addition to the graphical metamodel, additional constraints have to be enforced on the model. For example, one such rule states that data sinks are forbidden, i.e. *a data transformation must have both inputs and outputs.* Some or even most of these constraints could also have been specified in the graphical metamodel, at the cost of more cluttering the metamodel diagram. When developing a metamodel this is of course a tradeoff which must be evaluated on a case-per-case basis. The implementation of the well-formedness rules will be discussed in more detail in the next section.

3 Tool Support for the Metamodel

To really benefit of a SA/RT metamodel, tool support is required. We used the Software Modeling (SMW) toolkit [10] to automatically generate the metamodel, to create a SA/RT profile and, by using the scripting facilities of the tool, to provide automated querying and manipulation of SA/RT models.

3.1 The SMW Toolkit

SMW is built upon the OMG's MOF and UML standards, allowing editing, storage and manipulation of metamodels. The tool uses the Python language [11] to describe the elements of a model, each element being represented by a Python class. This fact provides the basic mechanism for accessing and executing queries over given models, as well as implementing transformations of the model elements in an OCL-like style. In addition, SMW allows the creation and usage of user defined profiles, based on the MOF standard.

3.2 SA/RT Metamodel Generation

When developing the metamodel we employed a graphical approach. The Python implementation of a specific metamodel can be generated simply by giving to the SMW metamodel generator the metamodel file as input as a UML class diagram saved in XMI [12] format. Therefore, by drawing the SA/RT metamodel class diagram directly into SMW we were able to automatically generate the metamodel.

The SMW toolkit enforces some constraints automatically (e.g., the multiplicity of the model elements) and adds checks for these in the metamodel file, but more specific constraints still have to be defined by hand in a separate file and supplied as input to the metamodel generator. The constraints were extracted from the informal specification of SA/RT and implemented as well-formedness rules coded directly in Python, using OCL-like constructs. The approach is similar to the way the UML metamodel is defined. Some examples of constraints, and their implementation in Python, are shown below. In total 20 such well-formedness rules were implemented to constrain the dataflow part of the SA/RT models. A complete list of these rules can be found in [9].

```
def wfrDataStore1(self):
  "A DataStore may only be connected to DataFlows"
  return(self.association.forAll(lambda ae:
    ae.association.oclIsKindOf(DataFlow)))

def wfrFlow1(self):
  "Flows may not have the same source and target elements"
  return(self.connection.forAll(lambda ae1,ae2:
    not(ae1.participant==ae2.participant)))
```

3.3   The SA/RT Profile

To be able to create, edit and manipulate models in a graphical environment, a SA/RT profile has been implemented in SMW. Two possible approaches existed to represent the graphical elements: to use the existing UML notations or to implement a new editor in SMW featuring the actual SA/RT notations. We followed the second approach. While some work was needed to implement the editor functionality for the SA/RT profile, the only change which had to be made to the metamodel was the inclusion, in the `Auxiliary` package of the metamodel, of a `PresentationElement` class describing the physical views of the `ModelElement`.

A screen shot of the resulting profile is presented in Fig. 3 (a). The system shown represents the top-level model (i.e. context diagram) of the Cruise Control system described by Ward and Mellor. The property editor for the currently selected element (i.e. `'0-Maintain-AutoSpeed'`) can be seen at the bottom of the screen. A refinement of the top-level diagram is presented in Fig. 3 (b), where the outer flows (from e.g., the context- or some other higher-level diagram) have been connected to the inner, refined transformations. The state machine corresponding to the `'1-MonitorEngine'` control transformation is presented in Fig. 3 (c).

One slight problem due to following the graphical construction approach was that although we used well-defined rules to specify those characteristics of the metamodel which are not defined graphically (i.e. in the XMI file), we still needed to implement those rules again in the SMW editor. For instance, although one of our well-formedness rules specifies that a `join` or a `split` must not be connected to both data and event flows, we still have to specify this rule explicitly in the part of the editor which handles connections between elements. That is, it is not sufficient to check if the well-formedness rule holds after the erroneous element already has been added to the diagram, but rather the user should be prevented to add the incorrect element at all.

Of course, it is also the case that some well-formedness rules cannot be applied to models which are under development. An example of this situation is the well-formedness rule stating that a non-abstract `DataTransformation`, i.e. a data transformation which is not refined by any other transformations, may only be connected to `DataFlows` and `PromptFlows`, not to regular `ControlFlows`. When designing a model it would be unpractical to apply this restriction, as we are likely to have some

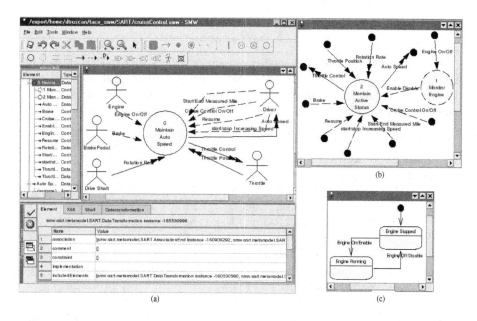

Fig. 3. Top-level DFD (a), its refined DFD (b) and the state machine of the *Monitor Engine* control transformation (c)

unrefined `DataTransformations` in our unfinished model which later are going to be refined, and thus become abstract. Figure 3 (a) illustrates this case, as here we have not yet added any refining transformations for the `'0-MaintainAutoSpeed'` trans-formation, but we still have control flows connected to it. Applying the well-formednes rule while designing the model would mean that we need to define all transformations completely before we can add flows between them. In this case it is thus more reasonable to only check that the condition holds for the complete model. The SMW editor features a shell through which the model can be inspected and also modified using Python scripts. Executing one single command in the shell window, all well-formedness rules on the metamodel are recursively checked.

4   Model Manipulation

Using the scripting facilities of the SMW tool, Python scripts could be implemented to navigate, query and manipulate SA/RT models. Next we present couple of examples of such scripts. For instance, the following script returns the name of all data flows in a model that are inputs for a data transformation element with a given name. Here, the function `getAllParts()` recursively returns all the elements of a given model.

```
dfdModel.getAllParts().select(lambda df:
    df.oclIsKindof(DataFlow) and
    dfdModel.getAllParts().select(lambda dt:
        dt.oclIsKindOf(DataTransformation) and
```

```
dt.name==someName and
df.connection[1].participant==dt)).name
```

Similar scripts can be used to modify or transform the SA/RT models created. One such example can be, for instance, when two output data flows with identical names originate in the same data transformation and have distinct target data transformations (sink). In this case a fork (clone) flow is added to replace the two flows.

```
dfdModel.getAllParts().select(lambda source:
   source.oclIsKindOf(DataTransformation) and
   dfdModel.getAllParts().select(lambda firstFlow:
      firstFlow.oclIsKindOf(DataFlow) and
      firstFlow.connection[0].participant==source~and
   dfdModel.getAllParts().select(lambda secondFlow:
         secondFlow.oclIsKindOf(DataFlow) and
         secondFlow.connection[0].participant==source and
         firstFlow.name==secondFlow.name and
         addAClone(firstFlow, secondFlow, source))))
```

In the same way, model transformations could be implemented not only between models of the same metamodel, but also between models of different metamodels (e.g., SA/RT and UML). Following, a partial example of a script that transforms a class diagram (i.e. umlModel) into a DFD (i.e. dfdModel) is presented. In there, each actor of the UML model is transformed into an external entity and added to the SA/RT model (lines 1-3). Similarly, the ≪control≫ and ≪interface≫ classes are transformed into corresponding data transformations and added to the DFD model (lines 5-8).

```
0. for el in umlModel.ownedElement:
1.    if el.oclIsKindOf(UML.Actor):
2.       ee=SART.ExternalEntity(name=el.name)
3.       dfdModel.ownedElement.append(ee)
4.    if el.oclIsKindOf(UML.Class):
5.       if el.stereotype[0].name=="interface" or
6.          el.stereotype[0].name=="control":
7.             dt=SART.DataTransformation(name=el.name)
8.             topEl.ownedElement.append(dt)
```

More details on these model transformations and how we used them to support a model-driven process were given in [5].

5   Conclusions

We presented a MOF-based meta-model for SA/RT. We described how the metamodel was constructed starting from the SA/RT specification and how it was implemented in the SMW tool. Using the metamodel, we were able to provide tool support for our model-driven approach presented in [5]. It allowed us to create and manipulate system models using both the graphical, as well as the scripting facilities of the SMW tool. In the same time, using OCL to enforce constraints of the SA/RT metamodel, gave us the possibility to verify and ensure the consistency of the models created.

Having the MOF standard as a common meta-meta-model for both SA/RT and UML meta-models, enabled us to easily combine and integrate the object-oriented and structured methods to represent views of the system under design at different steps of the development process and at different levels of abstraction. Moreover, it made possible to graphically create and manipulate, simultaneously and inside the same development framework, UML and SA/RT models of the system under design. In addition, benefiting of the scripting facilities of the tool and of the OCL-like constructions in Python, scripts to support model transformations between SA/RT models or between SA/RT and UML models could be implemented. They provided us the basic means for automation, thus speeding up considerably the development time and reducing the error-prone sources during the transition from one step to another.

The implementation of the SA/RT metamodel proved to be an important opportunity in experiencing the concepts of metamodeling and model-driven development, and in the same time, it served as a case study for the SMW toolkit, enabling us to evaluate the features and detect the shortcomings of SMW as a metamodeling tool.

A similar approach can be followed up to design other MOF-based metamodels in order to provide tool support for already existing notations or to integrate UML (or SA/RT) with other/new metamodels. This would result in an enriched set of tools available for the system designer. For instance, to benefit of existing UML profiles (e.g., UML/RT profile) one can use the approach to provide new descriptive features into SA/RT, like concurrency and timing information.

References

1. OMG: (Model Driven Architecture (MDA)) Doc. ormsc/2001-07-01 At www.omg.org.
2. OMG: Unified Modeling Language Specification, ver. 1.5. (Doc. formal/2003-03-01)
3. OMG: Meta-Object Facility (MOF). (Doc. formal/01-11-02 At www.omg.org)
4. Fernandes, J.M., Lilius, J.: Functional and Object-Oriented Modeling of Embedded Software. In: Proceedings of the Intl. Conf. on the Engineering of Computer Based Systems (ECBS'04), Brno, Czech Rep. (2004)
5. Tool Support for DFD-UML Model-based Transformations. In: Proceedings of the Intl. Conf. on the Engineering of Computer Based Systems (ECBS'04), Brno, Czech Rep. (2004)
6. Baresi, L., Pezzè, M.: Toward Formalizing Structured Analysis. ACM Transactions on Software Engineering and Methodology **7** (1998) 80–107
7. Ward, P.T., Mellor, S.J.: Structured Development for Real-Time Systems. Prentice Hall/Yourdon Press (1985) Published in 3 volumes.
8. Hatley, D.J., Pirbhai, I.A.: Strategies for Real-Time System Specification. Dorset House Publishing Co., New York, USA (1987)
9. Isaksson, J., Truscan, D., Lilius, J.: A MOF-based Metamodel for SA/RT. Technical Report 555, Turku Centre for Computer Science (2003)
10. Porres, I.: A Toolkit for Manipulating UML Models. Software and Systems Modeling, Springer-Verlag **2** (2003) 262–277
11. : (Python Programming Language) http://www.python.org.
12. OMG: XML Metadata Interchange (XMI) spec. (Doc. formal/00-11-02. At www.omg.org)

Modelling SystemC Process Behavior by the UML Method State Machines*

Elvinia Riccobene and Patrizia Scandurra

Dipartimento di Matematica e Informatica,
Università di Catania - V.le A. Doria,
6 - 95125 Catania, Italy
{riccobene, scandurra}@dmi.unict.it

Abstract. We describe the *SystemC Process State Machines* that we
have defined, as a variation of the UML method state machines, to model
the behavior of reactive processes of the SystemC language. They are
part of a complete UML 2.0 profile for SystemC that we have developed
to improve the SoC (System on a Chip) design flow in order to provide a
modelling framework which allows high-level designing SoC components
in the style of UML using the SystemC design primitives.

1 Introduction

The Unified Modeling Language (UML) [9] offers a variety of behavior specification mechanisms that differ in their expressive power and domain of applicability,
such as the state machine automata, activity diagrams in the style of Petri-net
graphs, informal descriptions in the form of use cases, etc. However, generating code from these diagrammatic descriptions is a challenging task due to the
dynamic nature of the specification formalisms, and because many of their modelling concepts are not directly supported by the object oriented programming
languages. So, a huge gap exists between high-level modelling languages and
programming languages.

We believe that, in order to bridge this gap between design and implementation and allow straightforward reduction of platform independent languages to
platform dependent languages – as conceived by the Model Driven Architecture
(MDA) [4] initiative –, solid mapping criteria (or transformation bridges) must
be established between languages. Moreover, we believe that additional styles of
behavioral specification – introduced through the extension mechanism of UML
profiles to better capture behavioral facets of particular target languages – are
valuable in that they raise the level of abstraction with respect to the target platform, and allow the definition of specific generative techniques able to produce
complete low-level implementation code directly from the design.

---

* This work has been partially supported by the project *Tecniche e metodologie di pro-
getto, documentazione, verifica e validazione per i sistemi di IP (Intellectual Property)* at STMicroelectronics.

N. Guelfi (Ed.): RISE 2004, LNCS 3475, pp. 112–121, 2005.

In this paper, we exploit the UML 2.0 method state machines [9] to model the behavior of reactive processes of the SystemC language [6]. We define a new graphical formalism, called *SystemC Process State Machines*, which allows high level specification of the functionality of the SystemC processes, and generation of efficient and compact executable SystemC code from the behavioral design. This demand has emerged in a research project targeting to define a UML 2.0 profile for SystemC[1] that we have developed to improve the SoC (System on a Chip) design flow with the advantages of high-level modeling SoC components in the style of UML using the SystemC design primitives, and of the full automatic generation of SystemC code.

In section 2 we sketch some basic fundamentals of the SystemC language, focusing in particular on the thread process behavior. In section 3 we introduce the basic definitions of a UML profile, and in 3.2 we describe the main stereotypes for thread processes. In 3.3 we present the SystemC Process State Machine which models the behavior of the SystemC thread processes. Related work and conclusions are given in sections 4 and 5.

2   SystemC Fundamentals

SystemC is an open standard controlled by a steering group composed of thirteen major companies in the EDA and electronics industries. It is one of the most promising system-level design languages intended to support the description and validation of complex systems in an environment completely based on the C++ programming language.

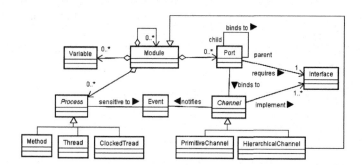

Fig. 1. A simplified SystemC Metamodel

Figure 1 depicts a simplified metamodel of the main SystemC terms and abstractions. SystemC has a notion of a container class, called *module*, that provides the ability to encapsulate *structure* and *functionality* of hardware/software blocks for partitioning a design of a system. A system is essentially broken down into a containment hierarchy of *modules*. Each module may contain *variables* as simple data members, *ports* for communication with the outside environment and *processes* for performing module's functionality and expressing concurrency in the system. Three kinds of processes are available: *method* processes, *thread* processes, *clocked thread* processes. They run concurrently in the design and may be sensitive to *events* which are notified by *channels*. A port of a module is a proxy object through which the process accesses a channel interface. The *interface* defines the set of access functions (methods) for a channel, while the channel provides the implementation of these functions to serve as a container to encapsulate the *communication* of blocks. There are two kind of channels: *primitive* channels and *hierarchical* channels. Primitive channels do not exhibit any visible structure, do not contain processes, and cannot (directly) access other primitive channels. A hierarchical channel is a module, i.e., it can have structure, it can contain processes, and it can directly access other channels.

2.1   SystemC Processes Behavior

Processes are the basic unit of execution within SystemC providing the mechanism for simulating concurrent behavior. They can be classified as `sc_method`, `sc_thread` and `sc_cthread`. Each kind of process has a different behavior, but all processes run *concurrently*. The process code is *sequential*, and not *hierarchical*, i.e. no process will call another process directly from code (processes can only cause other processes to execute by notifying event occurrences).

All processes are usually called (by the kernel scheduling process), all at once, at the beginning of simulation, and then each process is activated only on the base of its *static sensitivity* list, which consists of an initial list of zero, one, or more designated events that can dynamically change at run time realizing the so called *dynamic sensitivity* mechanism. Moreover, a process can be explicitly not *initialized* when simulation starts – a `dont_initialize` command statement following the process declaration in the module constructor declares that the process is not ready to run – , so it does not execute when simulation starts like other regular processes do, but it will execute after a first event occurrence of its static sensitivity (if any).

For lack of space, in this paper we focus on the `sc_thread` processes. The complete UML profile definition for SystemC can be found in [1].

SystemC Thread Process. A `sc_thread` process (thread process, in brief) behaves like a function with no arguments and no return type but with the additional ability to be explicitly suspended and resumed from where it was left when the notification of an event condition, that it is waiting for, occurs. A thread process remembers the point of suspension saving all local variables values (its internal state).

Thread processes may use static sensitivity, dynamic sensitivity or both, to which they should normally react. The *static sensitivity* is specified by a declarative list (possibly empty) of events on specific inputs ports determined before execution starts. The SystemC function `wait()` (with no arguments) is called by a process when it needs to suspend until one of the events of its static sensitivity list is triggered. The *dynamic sensitivity* mechanism is performed by the `wait(e*)` function calls executed by the process itself for specifying the event condition `e*` on which the process wishes to suspend: the static sensitivity list is temporarily overridden and only the notification of `e*` will cause the thread process to be resumed.

If the body or parts of the body of the thread process are required to be executed more than once, typically it is implemented with an *infinite loop*. This ensures that the process can be repeatedly reactivated. If a thread process does not have an infinite loop and does not call `wait(e*)` in any way, then the process will execute entirely and exit within the same *delta-cycle* (i.e. a very small step of time consisting of separate evaluate and update phases). Finally, if a thread process does have an infinite loop but does not have wait calls in any way, then the process will continuously execute and hence no other process will execute.

3   The UML Profile for SystemC Thread Processes

A UML *profile* is a set of *stereotypes* each of which defines how the syntax and the semantics of an existing metaclass of the UML metamodel is extended for a specific domain terminology or purpose. A stereotype can define additional *constraints* expressed as formula in the Object Constraint Language (OCL) [5] over its base metaclass as well as *tags* to state additional properties. A constraint is a semantic restriction of the extended modeling element within the UML. A tag is a user-defined property of a stereotype; the actual properties of the extended model elements are specified using tagged values.

For defining profiles, UML 2.0 is endowed with a standard graphical notation. A profile is denoted as a package with the keyword ≪*profile*≫. Within the profile package, a class of the UML metamodel that is extended by a stereotype is notated as a conventional class with the optional keyword ≪ *metaclass* ≫. A stereotype is depicted as a class with the keyword ≪ *stereotype* ≫. The extension relationship between a stereotype and the metaclass that the stereotype extends is depicted by an arrow with a solid black triangle on the end pointing toward the metaclass.

3.1   SystemC Module Stereotypes

A SystemC module is represented by a UML structured class with the stereotype ≪*sc_module*≫[1]. Its processes are statically declared within the module class as operations stereotyped by ≪*sc_method*≫, ≪*sc_thread*≫ and ≪*sc_cthread*≫ according to the nature of the process and with no return type and no arguments. The static sensitivity list of a process is represented as a tagged value **sensitive** introduced for the operation stereotypes (see section 3.2). The dynamic sensitivity of a process is, instead, captured at *behavioral level* by the operational semantics of the method state machine associated to the process

---

[1] This formalization reflects the nature of SystemC processes viewed as module functions.

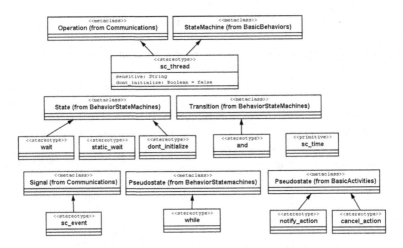

Fig. 2. SystemC Thread Process Stereotypes

(see section 3.3). A module containing thread processes is considered an *active* class, and it is shown by a class box with additional vertical bars.

3.2   SystemC Thread Process Stereotypes

We introduce here some stereotypes used in the next section for the thread process state machines capturing the semantics of the SystemC thread process behavior by means of the run-to-completion step semantics of the UML state machines. Figure 2 reports the stereotypes definition using the standard UML 2.0 notation [9] for writing profiles.

The stereotype `sc_thread` labels both the operation indicating the thread process in the operation compartment of the context module class, and the method state machine defined for the process (see next section). The tagged value `sensitive` is specified for declaring the static sensitivity list of the process (if any). In this case, the tagged value takes the form `sensitive = ` $\ll e_{1s} \ll$ `..` $\ll e_{Ns}$ where $e_{1s}, .., e_{Ns}$ are events. The boolean tagged value `dont_initialize`, whose default value is `false`, represents the the SystemC `dont_initialize` command statement in the process declaration[2].

The stereotypes `wait`, `static_wait`, and `dont_initialize` label simple states in a process state machine (see next section).

The stereotypes `static_wait` and `wait` model the SystemC `wait()` and `wait(e*)` calls for resuming a waiting process on the base of its static or dynamic sensitivity (if any), respectively. A `static_wait` state has only one outgoing transition, the *static resuming transition*, with no explicit triggers (similarly

---

[2] Note that, in case of processes not initialized, the state machine associated to the process contains a state with stereotype `dont_initialize` which captures the operational semantics of the command.

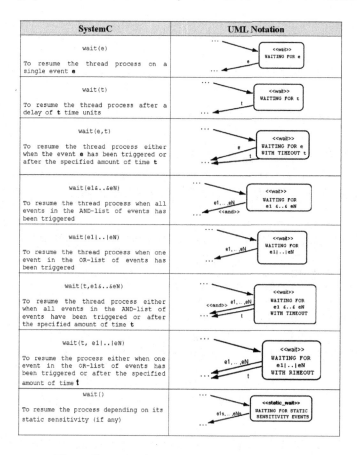

Fig. 3. Dynamic Sensitivity of a Thread Process

to a UML *completion transition*). We assume that the events of the static sensitivity list of the calling process are the implicit triggers of this transition, and that the transition fires when one of them is triggered. The event condition e* of a SystemC `wait(e*)` call is modelled as trigger of the outgoing transitions, the *dynamic resuming transitions*, of a `wait` state. The condition e* may have different forms. In Figure 3 we report the notation for all possible cases[3].

In a process state machine, the stereotype `dont_initialize` labels a simple state following the initial state of the top composite state. This state captures the operational semantics of the SystemC `dont_initialize` declaration for a process. A dont_initialize process does not execute when simulation starts, but after an event of its static sensitivity (if any) occurs. If there is no static sensitivity specified for the process, then the process will never execute. A `dont_initialize` state has only one outgoing transition with no explicit triggers; we assume that

---

[3] Note that $e_{1s}, .., e_{Ns}$ stand for the static sensitivity list of the thread process (if any).

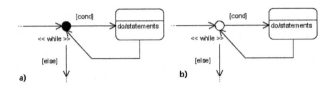

Fig. 4. While loop

the events of the static sensitivity list of the process are the implicit triggers of this transition, and the transition fires when one of the events occurs.

The stereotype **and** specifies the AND-semantics for the list of events labelling a transition: the transition fires when all the events have been effectively triggered. It is used to model the SystemC **wait** call with an AND-list of events. In fact, the stereotype **and** labels outgoing transitions of a **wait** state to guarantee that the process leaves the state **wait** when all events in the list have been triggered (not necessarily at the same time).

The stereotype **while** can be applied to a *junction* or *choice* pseudostate to model the conventional **while** loop of programming languages (see Figure 4). The infinite loop mechanism of a thread can be modeled with a **while** pseudostate with true condition on the outgoing transition. Choice pseudostates must be used in place of junction pseudostates whenever the head condition of the **while** loop is a function of the results of prior actions performed in the same run-to-completion step. In this case, in fact, the choice allows splitting of transitions into multiple outgoing paths such that the decision on which path to take may be a function of the results of prior actions performed in the same run-to-completion step.

We intentionally leave out the description of stereotypes for events and actions which are not essential to read the process state machines presented below. Further details can be found in [1].

3.3   SystemC Thread Process State Machine

In the UML profile developed for SystemC, the behavior of reactive processes are modeled by means of *SystemC Process State Machines* that we have defined as a variation of the UML *method state machines*. In the UML, a "method" state machine is a state machine which has an associated *behavioral feature* (i.e. a dynamic feature such as an operation) and it is the *method* of this behavioral feature, i.e. it specifies the algorithm or procedure for the behavioral feature.

Here we present the SystemC Process State Machine for sc_thread processes. A similar approach has been followed to define state machines for **sc_method** and **sc_cthread** processes.

For a SystemC thread process we can distinguish the behavior cases shown in Figure 5 on the base of the process sensitivity (static, dynamic or both), the process initialization, and the process termination. Every SystemC thread process behavior matches a specific *abstract behavior pattern*. The term "abstract" here denotes that the pattern, and therefore the method state machine associated

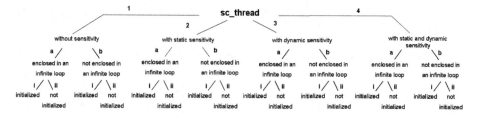

Fig. 5. Behavior cases for a SystemC Thread Process

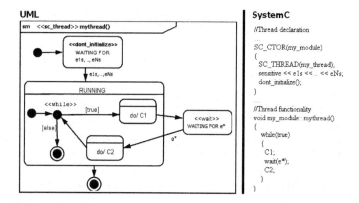

Fig. 6. A Thread Process State Machine

to the pattern, may be refined to add further details depending on the specific functionality of the process.

The left side of Figure 6 depicts an example of the abstract state machine pattern corresponding to a process matching the case 4.a.ii, namely a process: (i) having both a static (the list of events $e_{1s}, \ldots, e_{Ns}$) and a dynamic sensitivity (represented by the state WAITING FOR e* with the stereotype wait), (ii) running continuously (its functionality is enclosed in an infinite while loop), and (iii) not initialized (the stereotyped dont_initialize state follows the initial state). The state machine reflects the behavior of the thread process. Note that the notation used for the wait state in the state machine pattern given in Figure 6 stands for a shortcut to represent a generic wait(e*) call where the event e* matches one of the cases reported in Figure 3.

After created, the thread process does not execute immediately, but it stays in the stereotyped dont_initialize state; after an event of its static sensitivity list occurs, then it enters in the composite state RUNNING, continuously executing the same steps: first, it performs the activity C1[4] and waits until the awaited event e* is notified; then, it performs the activity C2, and, afterward, it restarts again.

---

[4] Activities C1 and C2 stand for blocks of sequential (or not) code without wait statements.

The corresponding SystemC pseudo-code, straightforwardly generated from the machine, is reported in the right side of Figure 6.

The pattern depicted in Figure 6 can be more complex in case of one or more `wait` statements are enclosed in the scope of one or more nested control structures. In this case, as part of the UML profile for SystemC, the control structures `while`, `if-then`, etc. need to be explicitly represented in terms of special stereotyped junction or choice pseudostates combined together in order to stand out the state-like representation of the `wait` calls. These stereotypes can be seen as an approach complementary to the UML action semantics very useful in practice to effectively generate code from state diagrams in a style that reflects the nature of constructs of the final implementation language, despite to well know techniques (like state pattern, stable table pattern, etc.) currently used to achieve this goal.

4   Related Work

In cooperation with industrial partners, UML has been deployed in real application scenarios which provided extensive experiences on how to use UML effectively within a system development process. The possibility to use UML 1.x for system design [2, 3] started already at Cadence Design Systems in 1999. However, the general opinion was that UML (before version 2.0) was not mature enough as a system design language, in particular if compared to others emerging system design environments.

Working jointly with Fujitsu Laboratories Limited, Fujitsu [7] has recently developed a new SoC design methodology that employs UML and C/C++/SystemC programming languages. The methodology differs significantly from the conventional LSI (Large Scale Integration) design methodology in two points: (a) the use of the UML to describe the specification; (b) the introduction of UML and C++/SystemC for the phases from the system partition into hardware and software components.

All of the known experiences based on the use of C/C++/SystemC languages have in common the use of UML stereotypes for SystemC constructs, but it seems that these are not included in an appropriate and standardized language of something like "UML Profile for SystemC". Moreover, all of the proposals are based on the previous versions of UML, UML 1.x, making difficult and little scalable the structural representation of systems without the architectural constructs offered by the UML in its new version 2.0.

The SysML Partners [8] are collaborating to customize UML 2.0 to define a modeling language for *systems engineering applications*, called Systems Modeling Language (SysML) [5]. Although SysML reuses the more mature second generation of UML, it has to be intended as a *general-purpose* modeling lan-

---

[5] *Systems engineering applications* include the specification, analysis, design, verification and validation of complex systems with both hardware and software components, personnel, procedures, and facilities.

guage – a Platform Independent Modeling (PIM) language, as conceived by the MDA [4] vision – for systems engineering applications. So it is in agreement with our UML profile for SystemC which is a Platform Specific Modeling (PSM) Language. Moreover, since SysML preserves the basic semantics of UML 2.0 diagrams (state formalism and interaction diagram, e.g., are unchanged), our UML Profile can be thought (and effectively made) a customization of SysML rather than UML.

5   Conclusions

In this paper, we explore in the context of a UML profile for the SystemC language, how particular extensions of UML state machines can be defined as "method" of "behavioral features" to completely specify the implementation of that features, i.e., the computations that generates the effects of the behavioral features when activated on event triggering.

The UML profile for SystemC defines a language that allows to analyze, design, construct, visualize and document the software and hardware artifacts in a SoC design flow. As future work, we are developing a tool set supporting the design flow. It should allow *models developing* using the SystemC UML profile, *models analysis* exploiting tools for visualization, simulation, transformation, and *models coding* by automatically linking the SystemC profile constructs to the language constructs.

Acknowledgment. We thank Alberto Rosti of the STMicroelectronics Agrate Lab Research and Innovation for having tested the UML profile to design SoC components and for his very useful suggestions and comments.

References

1. E. Riccobene, P. Scandurra, A. Rosti and S. Bocchio. A UML 2.0 Profile for SystemC. ST Microelectronics Technical Report, 2004.
2. G.Martin. UML and VCC. White paper, Cadence Design Systems, Inc, Dec. 1999.
3. G.Martin, L.Lavagno, J.L.Guerin. Embedded UML: a merger of real-time UML and co-design. In *CODES*, 2001.
4. OMG, The Model Driven Architecture (MDA). `http://www.omg.org/mda/`.
5. OMG, UML 2.0 OCL Final Adopted Specification, ptc/03-10-14.
6. The Open SystemC Initiative. SystemC. `http://www.systemc.org`.
7. Q.Zhu, R.Oishi, T.Hasegawa, T.Nakata. System-on-chip validation using UML and CWL. In *Proc. of IEEE/ACM/IFIP CODES*, 2004.
8. SysML Partners web site. http://www.sysml.org/.
9. OMG, UML 2.0 Superstructure Final Adopted Specification, ptc/03-08-02.

My Favorite Editor Anywhere

Hayco de Jong and Taeke Kooiker

CWI, Department of Software Engineering,
Kruislaan 413, 1098 SJ Amsterdam, The Netherlands
{jong, kooiker}@cwi.nl

Abstract. How can off-the-shelf editors be reused in applications that need mature editing support? We describe our editor multiplexer which enables interactive, application guided editing sessions using e.g. GNU Emacs and Vim. At a cost of less than 1 KLOC of editor specific *glue* code, both IDE builders and users benefit. Rapid integration of existing editors reduces application development cost, and users are not confronted with yet another foreign editor with its own learning curve.

1   Introduction

Many applications such as e-mail clients, instant messengers, web browsers, and programming environments provide editing facilities. Full fletched, off-the-shelf editing solutions such as GNU Emacs [1] and Vim [2] are readily available, but many application developers still choose to write their own editor. Some utility libraries (e.g. Java's JFC/Swing library) contain partial solutions in the form of reusable editing/widgets. Still, developing and extending your own editor to encompass the feature richness common in mature text editors is far from a *rapid* software engineering exercise.

Offering a single builtin editor obviously also condemns the user to this editor. This poses no problem as long as the editing sessions are brief, e.g. during login or password entry. But when the editor is used for lengthy (programming) sessions, being forced to use the keybindings dictated by an editor that is not your personal favorite can easily lead to frustration.

This paper describes how we reuse and integrate existing editors in a programming environment. Although our implementation is based on needs we have in our own environment, both the idea and most of the implementation can carry over to other projects. Basically, projects that need editing support for (structured) documents and where interactivity with these editing sessions is desirable, could benefit from the architecture we describe.

The plan of this paper is as follows. This section continues with some background, motivation and discussion of related work. Following, in Section 2 we describe how we coordinate simultaneous editing sessions, and we show the architecture used to deal with various editors. Section 3 describes some of the implementation details of the architecture: the MULTIPLEXER which orchestrates simultaneous editing sessions and the *glue* that is needed between the MULTIPLEXER and the various editor instances. We conclude with a summary of our contribution and some future work in Section 4.

N. Guelfi (Ed.): RISE 2004, LNCS 3475, pp. 122–131, 2005.

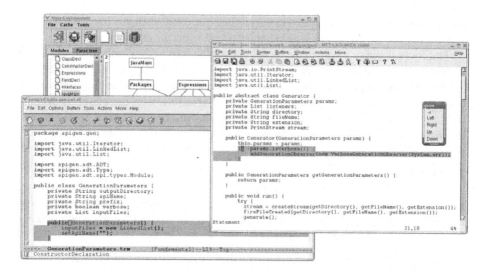

Fig. 1. GNU Emacs and Vim used simultaneously by an IDE

1.1   Background

The ASF+SDF Meta-Environment [3, 4] is a programming environment generator: given a language definition consisting of a syntax definition (grammar) and tool descriptions (using rewrite rules) a language specific environment is generated. Figure 1 shows a screenshot of the ASF+SDF Meta-Environment. A language definition typically includes such features as pretty printing, type checking, analysis, transformation and execution of programs in the target language. The ASF+SDF Meta-Environment is used to create tools for domain-specific languages and for the analysis and transformation of software systems.

The ASF+SDF Meta-Environment is used in several academic [5], industrial [6], and financial projects [7, 8]. Presently, the ASF+SDF Meta-Environment is intensively used in the software renovation oriented research project CaLCE: "Computer-Aided Life Cycle Enabling". This project is financed by the Dutch Ministry of Economic Affairs and aims at the development of tooling to improve the overall quality of systems deployed in the financial setting.

1.2   Related Work

Some applications (e.g. the KDE and Gnome window managers) allow the configuration of a *foreign* editor. Whenever a body of text needs to be edited, the application executes the configured editor and waits for the user to complete the editing session. During this session, there is no interaction between the main application and the foreign editor: the editing session is *unguided*. In some applications instantiations of external editors can be *embedded*. Some examples are KDE's filemanager `konqueror` and e-mail reader `kmail` which can embed instances of a specially crafted version of the Vim text editor. In these cases, the host application (`kmail`) encapsulates the editor (`kvim`) and shows its window as if the editor were part of the application. This gives the user the feeling that his favorite editor is integrated in the application, even when this integration is only visual and there is no real interaction between host application and editor.

Our focus is not so much on the *visual* integration achieved by embedding the editor instances. Instead we emphasize *functional* interaction *during* the editing session.

Another way to look at application-editor interaction is to look at the editor as the main application, and to view external tools as subordinates of the editor. Especially users of the Emacs family of editors find ways to link their e-mail reader, spell-checker, or other popular application into Emacs by writing support *glue* in Emacs LISP.

2   Design

In any IDE it is common to have multiple simultaneous editing sessions, as users start and finish editing, switching from one file to another. To take care of any administrative issues we have to deal with the following tasks:

Managing. Using multiple editing sessions needs administration of open sessions and addressing these editing sessions.

Executing. Supporting several editors almost certainly results in different startup procedures for each editor. We provide an open and generic architecture for supporting several editors.

Marshalling. We need full interaction with the supported editors, which means that data has to be transferred from the application to the editor instance and vice versa.

We first have a look at the requirements (Section 2.1) and then split the design into editor independent (Section 2.2) and editor specific (Section 2.3) details, and we show how the components connect (Section 2.4) to form our multiplexing editor architecture.

2.1   Requirements and Considerations

Given our experience with editing issues in the Meta-Environment (Section 1.1) we are interested in a solution with the following characteristics:

Noninvasive. We are strongly determined *not* to edit the source code of any particular editor itself.

Simple. Keep the number of methods in the editor interface low: 10 rather than 100 methods. Prefer implementation of these methods in established programming languages (e.g. C or Java), rather than the editor's (sometimes arcane) domain specific scripting language.

Open. Both in terms of *platform* and *language*:

- Platform independence: although designed for a Unix environment, the implementation should be independent of whether this is e.g. Linux, SunOS, or Windows/Cygwin;
- Language independence: the architecture does not dictate any particular programming language for the editor connectors.

From the Meta-Environment point of view, we are at least interested in the following interesting editor actions and events:

Menu. We want to add menu items in the editor which, when selected by the user, are forwarded to the environment where they are handled.

Cursor. Cursor positioning and text highlighting can be directed by the environment (model) and rendered in the editor (view).

Modification. The editor notifies the environment of any changes the user makes to the file.

Save/Load. The environment can request the editor to save its contents or re-read them from the file system.

We start out with this restricted set, but we keep the design open to allow for later extensions. The less demands, the more editors we can potentially support. If for example an editor offers no support to add user-defined menus, we cannot set them up from another application either. Although we *could* patch the editor sources to add menu support we deliberately refrain from doing so.

2.2   Editor Independent Design

The editor independent design describes a generic way to manage and communicate with editor instances. Without knowledge of the actual editor instance one can provide an abstract level of communication by defining a common interface which provides all necessary functionality to fulfill the requirements given in Section 2.1. A tool that implements this design takes care of managing editing sessions, including starting and shutting down sessions, and communication with these editing sessions. The MULTI-PLEXER described in Section 3.1 is a tool that implements this.

2.3   Editor Specific Design

Managing editing sessions can be done in a generic way, but actual communication and execution of editor instances has to be editor specific. This communication can be done in various ways. While Vim makes use of an arcane syntax based communication protocol via the commandline, OpenOffice for example can be controlled by using an extensive API. These differences lead to different design implementations for different editors. To prevent changes to the MULTIPLEXER for every editor that has to be supported we introduce a connector (see Section 3.2) mechanism which separates communication with the actual editor instances from managing the editing sessions. For each supported editor there has to be a corresponding connector. All editor specific communication details are known to this connector, while the MULTIPLEXER can be implemented in a generic way. The generic interface provided by the MULTIPLEXER has to be implemented by every connector.

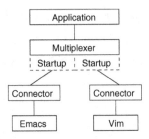

Fig. 2. Overview showing how editors are connected to an application

2.4   Execution Models

No two editor implementations are the same, and they are often written based on different designs. Editors based on the GNU Emacs philosophy prefer to interact with external processes only if they are executed by the editor. Other editors are more easily controlled by an external process.

We accomodate for this difference by allowing two execution models. Either the MULTIPLEXER first launches the connector which launches the editor, or the MULTIPLEXER launches the editor instructing it to immediately launch the connector.

Independent of the execution model, the final state is the same: the MULTIPLEXER communicates with the editor via a dedicated connector (Figure 2).

3   Implementation

Given the design from Section 2, we describe the MULTIPLEXER which contains the editor independent implementation in Section 3.1. This MULTIPLEXER invokes interface methods which in turn are implemented in editor specific connectors which are detailed in Section 3.2. Finally, we explain how we *glue* it all together in Section 3.3.

3.1   Editor Multiplexer

The editor MULTIPLEXER manages multiple simultaneous edit sessions by assigning each session a unique id. Subsequent calls to the edit session carry this id as one of the call's parameters. This allows the MULTIPLEXER to uniquely identify to which connected editor the request needs to be forwarded.

The MULTIPLEXER is currently implemented as a TOOLBUS tool, written in the C programming language. The TOOLBUS coordination architecture is a middleware layer with a process algebra based scripting language. Interested readers can find a comprehensive explanation of the TOOLBUS scripting language in [9]. Because the entire Meta-Environment architecture uses the TOOLBUS coordination architecture, making the MULTIPLEXER a TOOLBUS tool is the obvious choice. For applications that do not use the TOOLBUS, an implementation in the form of a C library would be equally feasible.

The choice for C as the implementation language was pragmatic. C offers direct access to operating system functionality such as process duplication through the use of the `fork` system call, execution of external processes using `exec` and has additional low level support for sockets, pipes and file descriptors. Although we also experimented with an implementation in Java during research in the context of connecting the Eclipse IDE editor [10], we opted for C's easy link to operating system functionality.

We show a simplified TOOLBUS interface definition of our MULTIPLEXER.

```
01  tool multiplexer is { command = "./editor-multiplexer" }
02
03  process EditorMultiplexer is
04  let
05    EM: multiplexer,
06    Editor, Filename: str,
07    SessionID, SL, SC, EL, EC: int,
08    MainMenu, SubMenu: str
09  in
10    execute(multiplexer, EM?)
11    .
12    (
13      rec-msg(edit-text(Editor?, Filename?))
14      . snd-eval(EM, Editor, Filename))
15      . rec-value(EM, SessionID?)
16      . snd-msg(edit-text(Editor, Filename, SessionID))
17    +
18      rec-msg(set-focus(SessionID?, SL?, SC?, EL?, EC?))
19      . snd-do(EM, set-focus(SessionID, SL, SC, EL, EC))
20    +
21      rec-event(EM, menu-selected(SessionID?, MainMenu?, SubMenu?))
22      . snd-msg(menu-selected(SessionID, MainMenu, SubMenu))
23    )
24    * delta
25  endlet
```

This example is limited to showing the execution (line 10) of the previously declared multiplexer tool (line 01). Following the execution is a looping construct (lines 12-24). During each iteration exactly one of the declared scenarios can occur. First, a request to start a new session is handled (lines 13-16). Second a request to set the focus to a particular region delimited by start-line, start-column, end-line and end-column (lines 18-19) to any existing editor can be handled. Finally, a menu event can come in from one of the connected editors (lines 21-22).

Applications that do not use the TOOLBUS, could use e.g. pipes, sockets or library calls to communicate with the MULTIPLEXER.

3.2   Editor Connectors

For each supported editor, we implement a small connector that translates the editor independent interface calls into the editor specific implementation. These connectors are necessary because each editor has its own unique scripting facilities or programming language (Vim uses Vim script, GNU Emacs uses Emacs Lisp), and because communication with each editor is usually handled in a slightly different way. We describe the connectors we implemented for Vim, GNU Emacs, and for a proprietary implementation of an editor in JFC/Swing.

Vim. The Vim connector is implemented partially in C and partially in Vim's scripting language. The C functions implement the text editor interface. Commands *from* the MULTIPLEXER *to* the editor are sent using Vim's remote scripting feature.

For example, the implementation of the `setCursor(int offset)` method looks like this:

```
01  static void gotoCursorAtOffset(int offset) {
02    char cmd[BUFSIZ];
03    sprintf(cmd, ":goto %d", offset);
04    sendToVim(cmd);
05  }
```

Events *from* the editor *to* the MULTIPLEXER, are initiated by Vim. E.g. Vim is instructed to forward buffer changes resulting from user editing by means of the Vim hook called `BufWritePost`:

```
01  func! EnableModificationDetection()
02    autocmd BufWritePost * :call BufModified()
03  endfunc
```

where `BufModified` is a function (in Vim script) that forwards this event to the MULTIPLEXER.

Currently, the editor specific glue for Vim is expressed in 501 lines of C code, and 77 lines of Vim script.

GNU Emacs. Similar to the `sendToVim` function, `sendToEmacs` is used to communicate from the MULTIPLEXER to GNU Emacs. The difference is that where Vim lacks a regular communication channel and we had to resort to using its remote scripting feature, with GNU Emacs we can communicate using a a pipe.

```
01  static void sendToEmacs(int write_to_editor_fd, const char *cmd) {
02    write(write_to_editor_fd, cmd, strlen(cmd));
03    write(write_to_editor_fd, "\n", 1);
04  }
```

The communication channel may be simpler in this version, but not all comes easy when dealing with GNU Emacs. The initial scripting necessary to setup the connector is programmed in Emacs LISP:

```
01  (defun init (args)
02    (setq emacs-connector
03      (let ((process-connection-type nil))
04          (apply 'start-process "emacs-connector" "*Meta*" "emacs-connector"
05            (split-string args))))
06    (set-process-filter emacs-connector 'multiplexer-input)
07    (process-kill-without-query emacs-connector)
08    (define-key global-map [mouse-1] 'mouse-clicked)
09    (add-hook 'after-change-functions 'buffer-modified () t)
10  )
```

Lines 02-08 execute the connector and register the LISP function `multiplexer-input` as input handler for the connector. Line 10 registers a mouse-click listener, and line 11 registers the `buffer-modified` function so it gets invoked whenever user editing causes the buffer to change.

Currently, the editor specific glue for GNU Emacs is expressed in 436 lines of C code, and 108 lines of Emacs LISP.

JFC/Swing Editor. As an experiment and possible extension to the Asf+Sdf Meta-Environment, we also created an editor based on the GUI classes available in JFC/Swing. Again similar to the previous implementations, we were able to connect this Java editor to the MULTIPLEXER. We do not show implementation details, but it is worthwhile to mention that the connection to this editor is based on sockets, rather than pipes (as we used for the GNU Emacs connector). Although we could have used the commonly accepted route where the standard input and output streams are sacrificed and used for communication via a pipe, we opted for the socket approach, just to add this route to our repertoire.

Currently, the editor specific glue for our JFC/Swing editor is expressed in 411 lines of C code, and a 5 line shell script to invoke java with the correct classpath for the editor.

3.3   Glueing It All Together

Now that we have the editor independent MULTIPLEXER, and the editor specific connectors, we can finally glue them together to get a working system. We describe how the MULTIPLEXER executes and communicates with an editor.

Executing an Editor. The MULTIPLEXER executes the requested editor as follows. For each editor, we write a small piece of (C) code that is loaded as a dynamic library. This mini library contains a single startup function with three parameters: the filename to be edited and the two file descriptors to be used for communication with the MULTIPLEXER. The startup function for the Vim editor looks like this:

```
01  void startup(const char *filename, int readFromFD, int writeToFD) {
02    char fromMultiFD[10], toMultiFD[10]; /* file descriptors as string */
03
04    sprintf(fromMultiFD, "%d", readFromFD);
05    sprintf(toMultiFD, "%d", writeToFD);
06
07    execlp("gvim-connector", "gvim-connector",
08           "--read_from_multiplexer_fd", fromMultiFD,
09           "--write_to_multiplexer_fd", toMultiFD,
10           "--filename", filename,
11           NULL);
12
13    perror("execlp:gvim/startup");
14    exit(errno);
15  }
```

The MULTIPLEXER invokes startup by using the dlopen and dlsym system calls (not shown here) for interacting with dynamic libraries. We thus *extend* the MULTIPLEXER with a single function per specific editor.

In the startup function, we choose one of the two execution models described in Section 2.4. For Vim we execute (lines 07-11) the connector, thus following the *connector first* execution model.

For GNU Emacs, we have a similar startup function. Only it was more convenient to execute emacs first and have it fire up the connector instead. GNU Emacs is then told to load the editor specific startup script (in this case written in Emacs LISP) and to begin by executing the function init:

```
01   void startup(const char *filename, int readFromFD, int writeToFD) {
02     char evalargs[BUFSIZ];
03     sprintf(evalargs,
04         "(init \"--read_from_fd %d --write_to_fd %d --filename %s\")",
05         readFromFD, writeToFD, filename);
06
07     execlp(EDITOR, EDITOR, filename, "-load", "gnu-emacs.el",
08         "-eval", evalargs, NULL);
...    /* error handling code omitted */
11   }
```

Communicating with an Editor. Depending on the functionality offered by each specific editor, we use different means of setting up a communication channel with the editor. We have used different channels ranging from a `pipe` (in GNU Emacs), to a `socket` (in the JFC/Swing editor), to the more esoteric remote scripting feature offered by Vim.

Independent of the type of the available communication channel, we use the *same* technique to *marshal* data over this channel. Instead of writing ad-hoc marshalling and de-marshalling code in the MULTIPLEXER and the connectors, we use APIGEN [11]. APIGEN takes as input an abstract data type description (ADT) and generates a C library or Java jar-file containing a.o. `set`, `get` and serialization methods.

Each command to and event from the editor is formalized in the text editor ADT. From this specification APIGEN generates the API implementation which we use to (de-)marshal communication between the MULTIPLEXER and editor.

4   Discussion and Future Work

We have implemented a framework that allows reuse of off-the-shelf editors such as GNU Emacs and Vim in the ASF+SDF Meta-Environment. By implementing as much as possible of this framework in a generic, editor independent way (our MULTIPLEXER), we can easily and rapidly add other editors to our environment. Deploying code generation techniques (APIGEN), and an available (programmable) middleware layer (TOOLBUS) ensures the solution is cheap in maintenance.

Our editing solution is *noninvase* (we never change any editor internals), *simple* (only a handful lines of code in the editor's own scripting language are needed), and *open*: our editing support has been tested on various Linux platforms, and we have both C and Java connectors.

Our editing framework was primarily designed for use in the Meta-Environment, which relies heavily on the TOOLBUS as its middleware layer. However, our contribution is not limited to using the TOOLBUS, and we plan to open up our results for use in a non-TOOLBUS setting, which we plan to offer as a downloadable package.

Another direction of interest is figuring out in which ways we can expand the text editor interaction. We have already experimented with syntax highlighting (i.e. one tool describes which part of the text gets which font attributes and colour and the rendering is done by the text editor), and structured editing, but conceivably several more applications can benefit from our support.

Obviously, the more complicated the things we demand, the less editors we will be able to fully support. Vim, for example lacks atomic functionality to colour a specific region of characters (although it does offer complex syntax highlighting). This leads to the following question: *what is the set of text editing primitives that is small enough to be covered by almost any editor, but large enough to be useful in most applications that require editing?*

Finally, as its name states, one of the MULTIPLEXER's task is *multiplexing* simultaneous editing sessions. In a coordination architecture such as the TOOLBUS, the multiplexing *concern* could be applicable to other tools as well. If this notion were lifted to a TOOLBUS primitive, any setting that launches multiple instances of a tool with the same interface could possibly benefit.

References

1. Stallman, R.M.: Emacs the extensible, customizable self-documenting display editor. In: Proceedings of the ACM SIGPLAN SIGOA symposium on Text manipulation. (1981) 147–156
2. Moolenaar, B.: Vim is a highly configurable text editor built to enable efficient text editing. Vim 6.3 is available for download from http://www.vim.org (2004)
3. van den Brand, M.G.J., van Deursen, A., Heering, J., de Jong, H.A., de Jonge, M., Kuipers, T., Klint, P., Olivier, P.A., Scheerder, J., Vinju, J.J., Visser, E., Visser, J.: The ASF+SDF Meta-Environment: a Component-Based Language Development Environment. In Wilhelm, R., ed.: Compiler Construction (CC '01). Volume 2027 of Lecture Notes in Computer Science., Springer-Verlag (2001) 365–370
4. Klint, P.: A meta-environment for generating programming environments. ACM Transactions on Software Engineering and Methodology 2 (1993) 176–201
5. van den Brand, M.G.J., Iversen, J., Mosses, P.D.: An Action Environment. In: Electronic Notes in Theoretical Computer Science, Elsevier (2004) to appear.
6. van den Brand, M.G.J., van Deursen, A., Klint, P., Klusener, S., van der Meulen, E.A.: Industrial applications of ASF+SDF. In Wirsing, M., Nivat, M., eds.: Algebraic Methodology and Software Technology (AMAST'96). Volume 1101 of Lecture Notes in Computer Science., Springer-Verlag (1996) 9–18
7. Klusener, S., Lämmel, R.: Deriving tolerant grammars from a base-line grammar. In: Proceedings of the International Conference on Software Maintenance, IEEE Computer Society (2003) 179–189
8. Veerman, N.P.: Revitalizing modifiability of legacy assets. Journal of Software Maintenance and Evolution: Research and Practice 16 (2004) 219–254
9. Bergstra, J., Klint, P.: The discrete time ToolBus – a software coordination architecture. Science of Computer Programming 31 (1998) 205–229
10. van den Brand, M.G.J., de Jong, H.A., Klint, P., Kooiker, A.T.: A language development environment for eclipse. In: Proceedings of the 2003 OOPSLA workshop on eclipse technology eXchange, ACM Press (2003) 55–59
11. de Jong, H.A., Olivier, P.A.: Generation of abstract programming interfaces from syntax definitions. Journal of Logic and Algebraic Programming (JLAP) 59 (2004) 35–61 Issues 1–2.

Combining System Development and System Test in a Model-Centric Approach

M. Born[1], I. Schieferdecker[1], O. Kath[2], and C. Hirai[3]

[1] Fraunhofer FOKUS,
Kaiserin-Augusta-Alle 31, 10589 Berlin, Germany
{born, schieferdecker}@fokus.fraunhofer.de
[2] Technical University-Berlin,
Franklinstr. 28/29, 10623 Berlin, Germany
kath@cs-tu-berlin.de
[3] Hitachi SDL,Yokohama , Japan
c-hirai@sdl.hitachi.co.jp

Abstract. In this paper we will present, how a model centric approach cannot only be used to rapidly develop the system but also at the same time to support the provision of the system tests which is an integral part of the overall system development. The key technology used to achieve this is a set of meta-tools which contains model repository generators and model transformer generators.

1 Introduction

Model centric development of software system has recently become an important software engineering strategy for handling the complexity and the increasing requirements to larger and highly distributed software systems. This phenomena can be observed in different domains, from telecom over public sector to automotive and defense. The fundamental idea of model centric development is to replace the programming language code as the main artefact in the development process by models. These models exist on different levels of abstraction throughout the development process. They are not independent from each other and have various relations like trace or transformation relations. These relations allow to establish and maintain consistent views on the system, spanning over different abstraction levels from requirements through specifications and test cases. Furthermore, the degree of development automation is substantially increasing through the consequent application of model transformations wherever possible.

Another important observation is that the overall resources which are spent for a development project are distributed to a large percentage (up to 70%) to the requirements/analysis phase and testing phase. Therefore, the model centric approach will only be a success if it is possible to reduce the development effort in exactly these phases without a lack of quality. The approach which we want to discuss in this contribution integrates the system design tightly with the development of system tests, starting at higher levels of abstraction.

Our architecture for system development follows the idea of the Model Driven Architecture (MDA) as introduced by the Object Management Group [17]. Within the

N. Guelfi (Ed.): RISE 2004, LNCS 3475, pp. 132–143, 2005.

MDA, models are classified into platform independent models (PIM) and platform specific models (PSM). The term platform in the MDA sense refers to wide spread integration platforms like J2EE [12], CORBA Components [18] or Web services as well as to domain specific platforms like Autosar [16] for the automotive domain. The idea of MDA is that PIMs can be automatically transformed into PSMs and programming language code can be generated from PSMs.

The test software can be modelled and developed in exactly the same way as the functional system software. Abstract testing artefacts are derived and modelled from the existing information in PIMs. These platform independent test models (PITs) can be transformed to platform specific test models (PSTs), potentially taking additional information from PSMs. Then, the programming language test code, i.e. the code of the test components of the test system, can be generated from the PSTs. This situation is depicted in Fig. 1, still completely independent from any particular modelling language, test language or programming language.

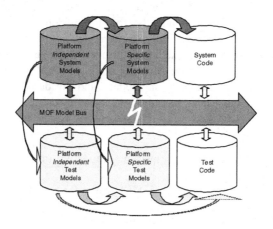

Fig. 1. The overall approach for combining system development and system test

In order to set up such an environment with concrete modeling, testing and programming languages, we apply a pattern which is used for each individual technique to be integrated. The pattern is applied for PIM, PSM, system code and for PIT, PST and test code. The pattern (Fig. 2) has the following steps:

- The modeling principles and relations of the modeling technique have to be defined.
- The modeling principles and relations have to be formalized in a metamodel.
- A notation for the modeling technique has to be defined.
- A process and guidelines of how to use the modeling technique have to be defined.
- Possible connections to other modeling techniques in the overall process have to be defined.

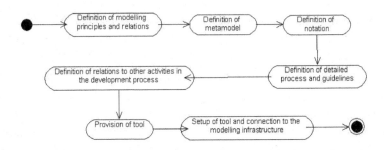

Fig. 2. Pattern for integrating modelling techniques into a modeling environment

- A tool has to be provided for the modeling technique.
- The tool has to be connected to the modeling environment.

In order to achieve practically an integrated modelling environment with the described process, at least the following technical facilities are required: A facility to store and access the models independently from the modelling tools used to present and manipulate them and a facility to transform models into each other. The first one is usually a repository, the second one a transformer or code generator facility.

In our approach we have used the Meta Object Facility (MOF [3]) as a formalism to describe the potential elements of models and to derive on one hand the repositories and on the other hand the transformers and code generators. The concrete techniques and tools we used for our integrated system and test development environment are:

- an open modelling tool-suite medini   (a MOF implementation [10]) for repositories and transformers,
- the Unified Modelling Language (UML) profile for Enterprise distributed object computing (EDOC [2]) with Rational Rose [7] for PIM modelling,
- the J2EE platform and Eclipse [8] for PSM modelling,
- the TTCN-3 technology [6] and Eclipse for the PIT and PST modelling and
- Java with Eclipse for coding.

These concrete technologies are used for an experiment to show the feasibility of our approach. The most challenging part of this experiment is the transformation of the PIM and PSM to the PIT and PST with the constraint, that the resulting test code must fit with the system code which comes from the PSM to code transformation. In this contribution, we will present our initial ideas on this subject.

The paper is structured as follows: We first introduce our medini toolset which provides the technology for tool integration via MOF repositories as well as a generic approach to model transformations. Then, we will show how the MDA based system development is done using EDOC and J2EE. After we have introduced the test development based on TTCN-3 we will discuss the transformations between the system models and the test models.

2   The Open Modelling Environment

The modelling environment that is used for the integration of development and test tools manages a set of model repositories based on MOF [3] and OCL (Object Constraint Language [4]) and provides means to access, store, read, and write models. The modelling environment is automatically produced by medini [10]. In Fig. 3, an overview of the modelling environment is depicted. The infrastructure forms an extendable bus containing a number of logically distinct repositories. System modelling and development tools are connected via their input and output pins to this model bus. The integration is achieved via model transformers.

Model transformers are based on the semantic definition of the modelling techniques. They operate on the model repositories. The skeletons for the transformer are themselves automatically generated with medini.

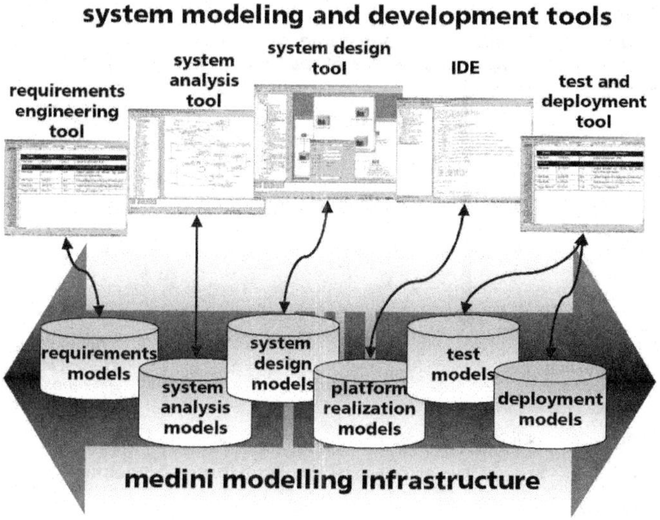

Fig. 3. Overview of the Open Modelling Infrastructure (medini)

2.1   Repositories to Store Models and Other Artefacts

In order to integrate a modelling technique into this modelling infrastructure at first, its modelling concepts need to be defined. That is, the semantics of each concept and the relations between concepts are defined in terms of a metamodel. This metamodel is the basis for the notation definition and for processes using artefacts of this modelling technique such as code generation from models. The processes are defined by use of model transformers. The notation, i.e. a human readable representation of a model, is used to present models to a user, e.g. a architects, modellers or developers.

Beside the conceptual advantages of separating between concept definition, notation definition and transformation rules, this approach has also a technical advantage: the modelling infrastructure can be directly generated from the metamodels independently of the particular notation or syntax for models.

2.2 Transformations Between Models in Repositories

Secondly, the relations of the newly integrated modelling technique to existing modelling techniques of the modelling infrastructure need to be defined in terms of model transformers. The medini model transformer generator is an engine to produce such transformers. A model transformation is defined as the transition of source model objects to target model objects, both representing (parts of) models in a concrete domain (e.g. UML [5], C++, Java, etc.). In a repository centric approach like the one presented in this paper, these models are maintained within externally accessible repositories. Since objects are connected by links, the source and target models are rather graphs than loose entities.

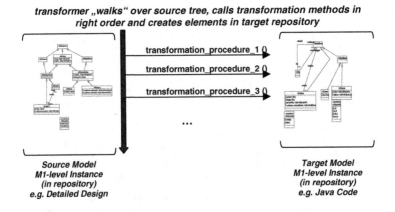

Fig. 4. Visualization of the Transformer Skeleton

To comprehend how a transformer works, it is essential to realize some requirements upon the process of transformation (see Fig 4). For each element in the source repository that is involved in a transformation, according rules must exist that accomplish the transformation task for this element. The rules may be combined in a fictive operation "do_transform" that contains the logic for the construction or modification of (a part of) the target model as result of a (set of) rule(s). Since model elements depend on each other, the call order of these transform operations is essential. This leads to a separation of the transformer into two parts: one part that iterates over a source model graph, i.e. the MOF level where system models are handled, and resolves dependencies between elements (the transformer skeleton, or "walker") and a second part that performs the transformation task corresponding to the rules defined on top of the metamodels.

3 System Development with EDOC and J2EE

In order to establish a concrete tool chain for system development (and later for system test) we apply the integration pattern described in Section 1 to provide an abstract PIM modelling technique, a platform (and by that a PSM) on top of which the software components of the system will be integrated, and a programming language, which is used to finally implement the system components. For the prototype, we have chosen EDOC [2] as PIM modelling technique, J2EE [12] as target platform and by nature Java [9] as the programming language. The tools to support the modelling are Rational Rose [7] and Eclipse [8].

The integration of EDOC with the modelling infrastructure is done as follows. At first, the modelling concepts for the EDOC modelling technique have been defined in a MOF metamodel. All EDOC modelling concepts, there various relations and the constraints which have to be fulfilled by each concrete EDOC model are formalized within that MOF metamodel. The metamodel for EDOC is already part of the EDOC specification, although some work was needed to make it MOF-compliant.

By applying medini to that metamodel, we obtain a MOF repository for the EDOC language with open interfaces to store, access and manipulate models in the repository by different clients. One client we connected to the repository is Rational Rose, where a plug-in realizes the EDOC UML profile. Hence, EDOC models can be defined by using Rose with the EDOC profile. They are stored in the repository and are ready for further processing. The generation of the EDOC repository from the EDOC metamodel and the connection of Rose with the EDOC UML profile are depicted in Fig. 5.

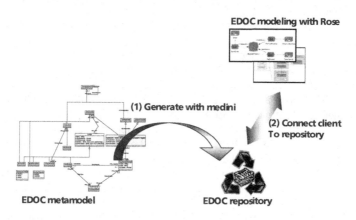

Fig. 5. Modelling with EDOC

The next step is to transform EDOC models – which are stored in the EDOC repository – to platform specific models (J2EE). For that, we have to define the target for the transformation and the transformation rules. Along our general approach, a metamodel for J2EE is needed to generate a J2EE repository. The transformation target is then this repository, filled by the EDOC2J2EE transformer. For the J2EE metamodel, we took the Java metamodel from Netbeans and extended it with the concepts of J2EE. Fig. 6 shows a sub model of the J2EE metamodel. The Java Class concept from the standard Java metamodel has been extended by the concept of Enterprise Beans and their interfaces.

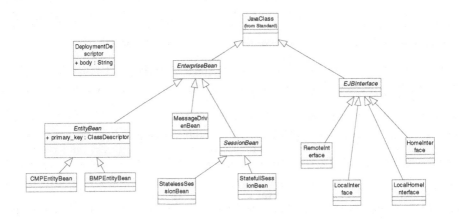

Fig. 6. Sub model of the J2EE metamodel

Once the repository is available, we can define the EDOC to J2EE transformation rules between repositories of the source and target models. The mapping rules concentrate in the initial version on the static parts of an EDOC model. Static EDOC models are comparable with UML 2.0 static structures: the basic concept of EDOC is that of a process component which communicates via ports to its environment. Process components can have a structure; they may be composed out of other components. At the ports of a process component, the communication is described either with flows (messages), operations, interfaces or structured into protocols which are used to group other communication elements together. There are special process components which are used to model entities and their relations in EDOC. The initial transformation rules of the mentioned EDOC concepts to J2EE are summarized in Table 1.

After the transformation has been performed by applying the transformation rules to an EDOC model in the EDOC repository, the generated J2EE model can be transformed to Java code which then can be deployed to a Java application server. We use Eclipse as Java development environment. Eclipse has an internal Java syntax tree which is automatically synchronized with the Java text files in the actual Eclipse project. Medini offers an Eclipse plug-in, which provides access for external clients to the Java syntax tree inside the Eclipse. To the outside, this plug-in behaves like a repository for Java. In fact, it offers exactly the API of a Java repository generated from the metamodel for Java without the J2EE extensions, i.e. it offers plain Java language constructs only. The only extension to the Java metamodel is the ability to attach Java doc tag information to Java language elements. This is because we use standard J2EE tools like Xdoclet and Lomboz [19] to generate all necessary artefacts for a J2EE application like deployment descriptors, configuration files etc. These tools expect Java sources with tags to generate the mentioned artefacts. Our tool chain contains another transformer which generates the Java sources with the proper tagging from the J2EE model in the J2EE repository. It uses the medini Eclipse plug-in as a target and the J2EE repository as a source. After being processed by Xdoclet/Lomboz, the application is ready for use.

Table 1. Initial transformation rules from EDOC to J2EE

EDOC Concept	J2EE concept
Process Component	Stateless session bean with remote interface and home interface,
Entity Component with primary key	Entity beans with fields and home interface
Contained process components	As process component but with local interfaces
Flows, Operations	Java messages as part of generated Java interfaces for their owning process components
Protocols	Java messages as part of generated Java interfaces, messages are recursively obtained from protocol structure (either operations, flows or sub-protocols)
Package	Java Package
Composite Data	Java class

4 System Test with TTCN-3

TTCN-3, the Testing and Test Control Notation [6][143], is the test specification and implementation language defined by the European Telecommunications Standards Institute (ETSI) for the precise definition of test procedures for black-box and grey-box testing. It is an extendible and powerful language, applicable to the specification of all types of reactive system tests over a variety of communication interfaces. TTCN-3 allows an easy and efficient description of complex distributed test behaviour in terms of sequences, alternatives, loops and parallel stimuli and responses. The test system can use any number of test components to perform test procedures in parallel. One essential benefit of TTCN-3 is that it enables the specification of tests in a platform independent manner. TTCN-3 provides the concepts of test components, their creation, communication links between them and to the system under test (SUT), their execution and termination on an abstract level, yet together with TTCN-3 execution interfaces to provide the realisation of concrete executable tests on different target test platforms. Features and capabilities being beyond TTCN-3 can be integrated into TTCN-3 by the use of external types, data and functions.

TTCN-3 offers various presentation formats to serve the needs of different TTCN-3 application domains and users. The programming-like textual core notation (see Fig. 7 left hand side) suits best programmers and test developers. The core notation can be developed within a text editor of the users' choice and enables an easy integration into an overall test environment. The graphical format of TTCN-3 is based on Message Sequence Charts (MSC) and aids the visualization of test behaviour. It eases the reading, documentation and discussion of test procedures and is also well suited to the representation of test execution and analyzing of test results. The tabular presentation format highlights the structural aspects of a TTCN-3 module and in particular of structures of types and templates.

Since TTCN-3 is an abstract test specification language it can be used both for the definition of PIT and PST models. However, TTCN-3 does not well integrate into the approach described in Section 1 as it has been classically defined in form of a formal syntax and a semiformal semantics. Therefore, a TTCN-3 metamodel has been developed beforehand [15].

The TTCN-3 test metamodel (see Fig. 7 right hand side) defines the TTCN-3 concept space with additional support for the different presentation formats. It does not directly reflect the structure of a TTCN-3 modules but rather the structure of the TTCN-3 language definition. It is defined as a single package with concept structures for types and expressions, for modules and scopes, for declarations and for statements and operations. ´

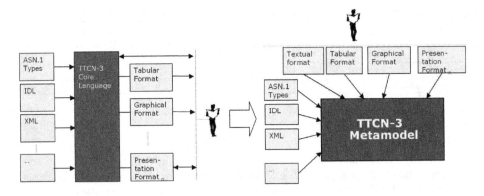

Fig. 7. The change to a metamodel centric TTCN-3 language architecture

This metamodel is the basis for the generation of test repositories and model transformers that take a system model and generate test models in TTCN-3. The meta-model for TTCN-3 language was technically realized by using the Eclipse Modelling Framework provided by Eclipse [1]. This allowed us to integrate not only test development and execution tools but also to integrate the development of system artefacts with the development of test artefacts as described in the following.

5   The Combined Approach

For the integration of the test development into system development, three transformations are of primary concern:

- The PIM (platform-independent system model) to PIT (platform-independent system tests) – in our case an EDOC to TTCN-3 transformation.
- The PSM (platform-specific system model) to PST (platform-specific system tests) – in our case a J2EE to TTCN-3 transformation.
- The PIT to PST – in our case a TTCN-3 to TTCN-3 – transformation taking into account the specifics of the EDOC to J2EE transformation.

In a first step, we concentrated on a structural PIM to PIT transformation. The transformation differentiates between process components/entities that need to be tested as part of the system under test (SUT) or that need to be emulated as part of the test system. Hence, the transformation is guided by the user which identifies the PIM parts being relevant for the test model. The default mapping for the main Component Metaclasses is given in the table below.

Table 2. Initial transformation rules from EDOC ECA to TTCN-3

EDOC ECA Concept	TTCN-3 Concept
PackageDef	TTCN-3 module
DataTypeDef	Data type definition to be used within the test system and to be exchanged via TSI
CompositeDataDef	Data type definition to be used within the test system and to be exchanged via TSI, which are basically record structures with flattened inheritance
ProcessComponentDef	Component type definition (with ports per interface)
DataManager	Component type definition (with local composite data variable)
Entity	Component type definition (with local composite data variable)
Port Classes	Port type definition

The transformation considers network sharable components only as those can be selected as a target for testing. Basically, the transformation does not consider containment hierarchies in the SUT as these are not visible from outside when using a black-box test approach. If however contained process components or entities are CUTs (components under test), then they need to be addressed within the SUT via the TTCN-3 address type. On the other side, if contained components are part of the test system and their behaviour is emulated, then they are mapped to separate test components interacting with test components representing process components or entities on higher level. Details of the port mapping are given in Table 3. Ports of CUTs or the test system are basically handled the same.

The approach of generating test models from system models follows the basic principles outlined in [13] and [1]. Initially, the structural aspects of test generation, i.e. types, test components and their test configurations, have been considered only. In a second step, behavioural aspects of the tests will be addressed. For that, we will analyse how the EDOC protocol can be used as a basis for the behaviour of PITs. Basically, established test generation techniques used for the derivation of tests from finite state machines (represented by UML state charts) or message sequence charts (represented by UML interaction diagrams) will be used. The first uses mainly state or transition coverage methods, while the second uses branch or path coverage methods to derive the various test sequences.

Still, the model transformers will generate basically test skeletons which need to be completed manually before they can be transformed into executable tests in Java and executed by use of the Testing Technologies' TTCN-3 tool set [11].

Table 3. Initial transformation rules from EDOC ECA Ports to TTCN-3

EDOC ECA Port Concept	TTCN-3 Concept
Synchronous port attribute	Procedure-based port
Asynchronous port attribute	Message-based port
Protocol port	In test system: message-based port plus test component representing the protocol behaviour In SUT: message-based port only
Port direction	Data types to be assigned to in, out our inout direction of a port
Flow port	Procedure- or message-based port
Flow port: process component properties	Additional signature for setting and getting of properties
Operation port	Signatures
Multi-ports	In test system: a test component with ports for all coordinated interfaces In SUT: all coordinated interfaces are part of TSI (or are addressed via TTCN-3 address)
Interfaces	Port types (possibly also test component)

6 Conclusion

This paper presents a general approach of integrating modelling and development techniques for systems and tests into a modelling infrastructure. The integration is done via metamodels representing the concept space of the techniques. The metamodels are the basis to generate repositories and to manage, access and manipulate models. In addition, they are used as source and target for model transformers, which define the relations between techniques integrated into the modelling infrastructure.

In a first step, we applied the modelling infrastructure to setup a development for EDOC. J2EE and Java on the system side and TTCN-3 and Java on the testing side. In a next step, the UML 2.0 testing profile (U2TP [1]) will be used for PITs instead of TTCN-3. The current restriction to focus on TTCN-3 only, is due to the unavailability of U2TP tooling. U2TP is an extension of UML 2.0 5 being based upon the UML metamodel. It follows the same fundamental principles of UML in that it provides concepts for the structural aspects of testing such as the definition of test components, test contexts and test system interfaces, and behavioural aspects of testing such as the definition of test procedures, test setup, execution and evaluation. The core UML is the basis for modelling and describing test artefacts. However, as software testing is based on a number of special test-related concepts these are provided by the testing profile as extensions to UML. U2TP is closer to the system modelling with the EDOC Profile for UML and will therefore be considered in our future work.

Acknowledgment

Part of the work described in this paper has been done within the context of the FP6/2003/IST/2 project Modelware which is partially funded by the European Commission.

References

1. Object Management Group: OMG ptc/04-04-02: UML 2.0 Testing Profile, Finalized Specification.
2. Object Management Group: OMG ptc/02-02-05: UML Profile for EDOC Final Adopted Specification.
3. Object Management Group: OMG ptc/03-10-04: MOF 2.0 Core Final Adopted Specification.
4. Object Management Group: OMG ptc/03-10-14: UML 2.0 OCL Final Adopted Specification.
5. Object Management Group: OMG ptc/03-08-02: UML 2.0 Superstructure Final Adopted Specification.
6. ETSI European Standard (ES) 201 873-1 version 2.2.1 (2003-02): The Testing and Test Control Notation version 3 (TTCN-3); Part 1: TTCN-3 Core Language. Also published as ITU-T Recommendation Z.140.
7. IBM/Rational: http://www-306.ibm.com/software/awdtools/developer/rose/
8. Eclipse: Open Source Integrated Development Environment, www.eclipse.org.
9. Java: www.java.org
10. IKV++ Technologies AG: http://www.ikv.de/medini/.
11. Testing Technologies: TTCN-3 tool set, www.testingtech.de.
12. Sun Microsystems: Java 2 Platform, Enterprise Edition , http://java.sun.com/j2ee/.
13. I. Schieferdecker, Z.R. Dai, J. Grabowski, A. Rennoch. The UML 2.0 Testing Profile and its Relation to TTCN-3. Testing of Communicating Systems (Editors: D. Hogrefe, A. Wiles). Proc. of the 15th IFIP Intern. Conf. on Testing of Communicating Systems (TestCom2003), LNCS 2644, Springer, May 2003, pp. 79-94.
14. J. Grabowski, D. Hogrefe, G. Réthy, I. Schieferdecker, A. Wiles, C. Willcock. An Introduction into the Testing and Test Control Notation (TTCN-3). Computer Networks, Volume 42, Issue 3, Elsevier, June 2003.
15. I. Schieferdecker,. G. Din: A Metamodel for TTCN-3. 1st Intern. Workshop on Integrated Test Methodologies. Colocated with 24th Intern. Conference on Formal Description Techniques (FORTE 2004), Toledo, Spain, Sept. 2004.
16. Autosar: http://www.autosar.org/.
17. Object Management Group: Model Driven Architecture, http://www.omg.org/mda/.
18. Object Management Group: CORBA Component Model, OMG document formal/2002-06-65.
19. Lomboz: http://forge.objectweb.org/projects/lomboz.

Author Index

Lecture Notes in Computer Science

For information about Vols. 1–3381

please contact your bookseller or Springer

Vol. 3439: R.H. Deng, F. Bao, H. Pang, J. Zhou (Eds.), Information Security Practice and Experience. XII, 424 pages. 2005.

Vol. 3437: T. Gschwind, C. Mascolo (Eds.), Software Engineering and Middleware. X, 245 pages. 2005.

Vol. 3436: B. Bouyssounouse, J. Sifakis (Eds.), Embedded Systems Design. XV, 492 pages. 2005.

Vol. 3434: L. Brun, M. Vento (Eds.), Graph-Based Representations in Pattern Recognition. XII, 384 pages. 2005.

Vol. 3433: S. Bhalla (Ed.), Databases in Networked Information Systems. VII, 319 pages. 2005.

Vol. 3432: M. Beigl, P. Lukowicz (Eds.), Systems Aspects in Organic and Pervasive Computing - ARCS 2005. X, 265 pages. 2005.

Vol. 3431: C. Dovrolis (Ed.), Passive and Active Network Measurement. XII, 374 pages. 2005.

Vol. 3429: E. Andres, G. Damiand, P. Lienhardt (Eds.), Discrete Geometry for Computer Imagery. X, 428 pages. 2005.

Vol. 3427: G. Kotsis, O. Spaniol (Eds.), Wireless Systems and Mobility in Next Generation Internet. VIII, 249 pages. 2005.

Vol. 3423: J.L. Fiadeiro, P.D. Mosses, F. Orejas (Eds.), Recent Trends in Algebraic Development Techniques. VIII, 271 pages. 2005.

Vol. 3422: R.T. Mittermeir (Ed.), From Computer Literacy to Informatics Fundamentals. X, 203 pages. 2005.

Vol. 3421: P. Lorenz, P. Dini (Eds.), Networking - ICN 2005, Part II. XXXV, 1153 pages. 2005.

Vol. 3420: P. Lorenz, P. Dini (Eds.), Networking - ICN 2005, Part I. XXXV, 933 pages. 2005.

Vol. 3419: B. Faltings, A. Petcu, F. Fages, F. Rossi (Eds.), Constraint Satisfaction and Constraint Logic Programming. X, 217 pages. 2005. (Subseries LNAI).

Vol. 3418: U. Brandes, T. Erlebach (Eds.), Network Analysis. XII, 471 pages. 2005.

Vol. 3416: M. Böhlen, J. Gamper, W. Polasek, M.A. Wimmer (Eds.), E-Government: Towards Electronic Democracy. XIII, 311 pages. 2005. (Subseries LNAI).

Vol. 3415: P. Davidsson, B. Logan, K. Takadama (Eds.), Multi-Agent and Multi-Agent-Based Simulation. X, 265 pages. 2005. (Subseries LNAI).

Vol. 3414: M. Morari, L. Thiele (Eds.), Hybrid Systems: Computation and Control. XII, 684 pages. 2005.

Vol. 3412: X. Franch, D. Port (Eds.), COTS-Based Software Systems. XVI, 312 pages. 2005.

Vol. 3411: S.H. Myaeng, M. Zhou, K.-F. Wong, H.-J. Zhang (Eds.), Information Retrieval Technology. XIII, 337 pages. 2005.

Vol. 3410: C.A. Coello Coello, A. Hernández Aguirre, E. Zitzler (Eds.), Evolutionary Multi-Criterion Optimization. XVI, 912 pages. 2005.

Vol. 3409: N. Guelfi, G. Reggio, A. Romanovsky (Eds.), Scientific Engineering of Distributed Java Applications. X, 127 pages. 2005.

Vol. 3408: D.E. Losada, J.M. Fernández-Luna (Eds.), Advances in Information Retrieval. XVII, 572 pages. 2005.

Vol. 3407: Z. Liu, K. Araki (Eds.), Theoretical Aspects of Computing - ICTAC 2004. XIV, 562 pages. 2005.

Vol. 3406: A. Gelbukh (Ed.), Computational Linguistics and Intelligent Text Processing. XVII, 829 pages. 2005.

Vol. 3404: V. Diekert, B. Durand (Eds.), STACS 2005. XVI, 706 pages. 2005.

Vol. 3403: B. Ganter, R. Godin (Eds.), Formal Concept Analysis. XI, 419 pages. 2005. (Subseries LNAI).

Vol. 3402: M. Daydé, J.J. Dongarra, V. Hernández, J.M.L.M. Palma (Eds.), High Performance Computing for Computational Science - VECPAR 2004. XI, 732 pages. 2005.

Vol. 3401: Z. Li, L.G. Vulkov, J. Waśniewski (Eds.), Numerical Analysis and Its Applications. XIII, 630 pages. 2005.

Vol. 3399: Y. Zhang, K. Tanaka, J.X. Yu, S. Wang, M. Li (Eds.), Web Technologies Research and Development - APWeb 2005. XXII, 1082 pages. 2005.

Vol. 3398: D.-K. Baik (Ed.), Systems Modeling and Simulation: Theory and Applications. XIV, 733 pages. 2005. (Subseries LNAI).

Vol. 3397: T.G. Kim (Ed.), Artificial Intelligence and Simulation. XV, 711 pages. 2005. (Subseries LNAI).

Vol. 3396: R.M. van Eijk, M.-P. Huget, F. Dignum (Eds.), Agent Communication. X, 261 pages. 2005. (Subseries LNAI).

Vol. 3395: J. Grabowski, B. Nielsen (Eds.), Formal Approaches to Software Testing. X, 225 pages. 2005.

Vol. 3394: D. Kudenko, D. Kazakov, E. Alonso (Eds.), Adaptive Agents and Multi-Agent Systems II. VIII, 313 pages. 2005. (Subseries LNAI).

Vol. 3393: H.-J. Kreowski, U. Montanari, F. Orejas, G. Rozenberg, G. Taentzer (Eds.), Formal Methods in Software and Systems Modeling. XXVII, 413 pages. 2005.

Vol. 3392: D. Seipel, M. Hanus, U. Geske, O. Bartenstein (Eds.), Applications of Declarative Programming and Knowledge Management. X, 309 pages. 2005. (Subseries LNAI).

Vol. 3391: C. Kim (Ed.), Information Networking. XVII, 936 pages. 2005.

Vol. 3390: R. Choren, A. Garcia, C. Lucena, A. Romanovsky (Eds.), Software Engineering for Multi-Agent Systems III. XII, 291 pages. 2005.

Vol. 3389: P. Van Roy (Ed.), Multiparadigm Programming in Mozart/Oz. XV, 329 pages. 2005.

Vol. 3388: J. Lagergren (Ed.), Comparative Genomics. VII, 133 pages. 2005. (Subseries LNBI).

Vol. 3387: J. Cardoso, A. Sheth (Eds.), Semantic Web Services and Web Process Composition. VIII, 147 pages. 2005.

Vol. 3386: S. Vaudenay (Ed.), Public Key Cryptography - PKC 2005. IX, 436 pages. 2005.

Vol. 3385: R. Cousot (Ed.), Verification, Model Checking, and Abstract Interpretation. XII, 483 pages. 2005.

Vol. 3383: J. Pach (Ed.), Graph Drawing. XII, 536 pages. 2005.

Vol. 3382: J. Odell, P. Giorgini, J.P. Müller (Eds.), Agent-Oriented Software Engineering V. X, 239 pages. 2005.